Anti Inflammatory Diet Cookbook for Beginners

Eat Tasty and Healthily To Prevent Inflammatory Diseases, Get a Healthy Body, Balance the Hormonal System, and Boost Fertility

By

Aurora Pope

I wrote this book using all my knowledge gained over years of work and my passion for cooking simple, healthy, and tasty recipes.

To thank you for trusting me, I thought I'd add four secret bonuses that you'll find inside the book.

 Private FB group with tips, new recipes, challenge participants, exercises

 Weekly planner and shopping list – save budget

 E-book challenge 30 days to get back in shape

 Light exercise plan eBook

TABLE OF CONTENT

INTRODUCTION 1

CHAPTER 1: ANTI-INFLAMMATORY DIET 2

CHAPTER 2: "ITALIAN WAY" INSTRUCTIONS FOR USE 4

CHAPTER 3: BREAKFAST RECIPES 7

    FERTILITY-BOOSTING PUDDING PARFAIT 8

    ANTI-INFLAMMATORY SMOOTHIE 9

    CHAMOMILE AND MAPLE PORRIDGE 9

    MEXICAN BREAKFAST HASH 10

    CHIA PUDDING 10

    HOMEMADE MUESLI 11

    FRESH TURMERIC SMOOTHIE BOWL 12

    SWEET POTATO TOASTS 12

    SOUTHWEST TOFU SCRAMBLE 13

    BABY KALE BREAKFAST SALAD WITH QUINOA & STRAWBERRIES 14

    PARSLEY FRITTATA 14

    OATMEAL WITH TURMERIC POWDER 15

    ZUCCHINI OATMEAL 15

    APPLE-CINNAMON OVERNIGHT OATS 16

    SPANISH OMELET 16

Chapter 4: Appetizer Recipes 17

    SWEET POTATO SOUP 18

    TOMATO & GREENS SALAD 18

    BROCCOLI WITH GARLIC AND LEMON 19

    QUINOA AND VEGETABLE SOUP 19

    BEET HUMMUS 20

    ASPARAGUS & SNAP PEA SALAD WITH CRISPY PROSCIUTTO 20

    OATMEAL CRACKERS 21

    GRILLED EGGPLANT PROVOLONE 22

    MIXED FRUIT SALAD 22

    VEGAN KIMCHI 23

    GRILLED TOMATOES 24

    BEET SALAD 24

    WINTER ORANGE & FENNEL SALAD 25

    PARSLEY SAUCE 25

    CELERY ROOT SALAD 25

Chapter 5: First Courses 26

Meat Recipes 26

| TURMERIC LIME CHICKEN .... 27 |
| CHICKEN, AVOCADO & QUINOA BOWLS WITH HERB DRESSING .... 28 |
| WHITE BEAN AND CHICKEN CHILI BLANCA .... 29 |
| PULLED PORK .... 29 |
| ROASTED CHICKEN WITH BALSAMIC VINAIGRETTE .... 30 |
| SWEET & SOUR CHICKEN .... 31 |
| TURKEY SHEPHERD'S PIE. .... 32 |
| CHEESY BROCCOLI CHICKEN RICE .... 33 |

Seafood Recipes 34

| BLACKENED SALMON .... 35 |
| GARLIC SHRIMP AND ASPARAGUS WITH ZUCCHINI NOODLES .... 35 |
| SUPERFOOD BAKED SALMON .... 36 |
| ROASTED SALMON, SMOKY CHICKPEAS, AND GREENS .... 37 |
| SHEET PAN TURMERIC SALMON WITH CHERRY SAUCE .... 38 |
| CREAMY SUNDRIED TOMATO PAN SEARED SOLE .... 38 |
| FISH CEVICHE .... 39 |
| THAI GREEN CURRY WITH SHRIMP AND KALE .... 40 |

Vegetable Recipes 41

| VEGAN ROASTED PUMPKIN CURRY .... 42 |
| RATATOUILLE .... 43 |
| CURRY TOFU .... 43 |
| CARROT GINGER SOUP .... 44 |
| CUMIN ZUCCHINI RINGS .... 45 |
| BROCCOLI SOUP .... 45 |
| INSTANT POT POTATO LEEK SOUP .... 46 |
| SORREL SOUP .... 47 |

Chapter 6: Main Courses 48

Meat Recipes 48

| CHICKEN TERIYAKI RICE .... 49 |
| SLOW COOKER DAIRY-FREE BUTTER CHICKEN .... 50 |
| BOILED CHICKEN .... 50 |
| GRILLED CURRY CHICKEN .... 51 |
| BEEFY BAKE CASSEROLE .... 51 |
| KUNG PAO CHICKEN .... 52 |
| CHICKEN PICCATA WITH GARLICKY GREENS & NEW POTATOES .... 53 |
| APPLE CIDER VINEGAR CHICKEN .... 54 |

Seafood Recipes 55

   MANGO SHRIMP KEBABS 56

   SALMON CHOWDER 56

   GARLIC SALMON 57

   CILANTRO LIME CATFISH 57

   ROASTED ORANGE-FENNEL STRIPED BASS 58

   CUMIN-CRUSTED SABLEFISH 59

   CREAMY LEEK AND SALMON SOUP 59

   ZOODLES & GRILLED SHRIMP WITH THE LEMON BASIL DRESSING 60

Vegetable Recipes 61

   CURRIED CHICKPEA LETTUCE WRAPS 62

   MEDITERRANEAN GRILLED EGGPLANT SALAD 63

   SWEET POTATOES WITH SWISS CHARD 63

   RED BEET BORSCHT 64

   SAUTÉED GREENS WITH FENNEL 65

   STUFFED PEPPERS 65

   STIR-FRIED ASPARAGUS WITH BELL PEPPERS AND CASHEW NUTS 66

   VEGAN TACOS 67

Chapter 7: Desserts 68

   PUMPKIN BALLS 69

   MANGO PUDDING 69

   APPLE CHIPS 69

   STRAWBERRY SHORTBREADS 70

   FRESH FIG & BANANA SMOOTHIE 70

   GINGERBREAD DESSERT HUMMUS 71

   WATERMELON PIZZA 71

   CHOCOLATE AVOCADO PUDDING 72

   PINEAPPLE SORBE 72

   KIWI SORBET 73

   EASY ROASTED FRUIT 73

   ALMOND BUTTER AVOCADO FUDGSICLES 74

   GUAVA SMOOTHIE 75

   ORANGE GINGER TURMERIC SMOOTHIE 75

   TURMERIC APPLE CIDER GINGER GUMMIES 76

Chapter 8: Between Meals 77

Snacks 77

   GRAIN-FREE BANANA GINGER BARS 78

   GARLIC PLANTAIN CHIPS 78

PUMPKIN PIE GRANOLA 79

MINTED BABA GHANOUSH 79

BLACK BEAN BROWNIES 80

NUTS AND SEEDS TRAIL MIX 80

SLOW COOKER APPLESAUCE 81

GRILLED EGGPLANT PROVOLONE 81

Aperitifs **82**

TANGERINE GINGER JUICE 83

CELERY JUICE 83

DILUTED APPLE CIDER VINEGAR 83

CUCUMBER WATER 84

APPLE-CINNAMON FLAVORED WATER 84

GREEN JUICE 84

BEET AND APPLE JUICE BLEND 85

STRAWBERRY SORBET 85

Herbal Teas **86**

PEPPERMINT TEA 87

ALMOND TEA 87

CHAMOMILE TEA 87

TURMERIC TEA 88

HERBAL TEA 88

LEMON GRASS TEA 89

PEACH TEA 89

JASMINE TEA 89

Herbs **90**

ITALIAN SEASONING 91

ALL-PURPOSE NO-SALT SEASONING MIX 91

GARLIC-HERB SEASONING 92

POULTRY SEASONING 92

ANTI-INFLAMMATORY OIL 92

SAMBAL OELEK 93

HOT KETCHUP 93

MUSTARD DRESSING 93

CONCLUSION **94**

4 WEEKS MEAL PLAN **95**

Measuring Conversions **101**

BONUS **105**

INTRODUCTION

Your body's natural response to wounds, diseases, and infections is inflammation. The signs of inflammation include redness, heat, discomfort, and swelling. However, other disorders have no symptoms at all.

If you suffer from inflammatory conditions, your diet should change to anti-inflammatory. Examples include active hepatitis, chronic peptic ulcer, rheumatoid arthritis, asthma, Crohn's disease, sinusitis, Endometriosis, periodontitis, and other conditions. In addition to medical care, a healthy diet is crucial. An anti-inflammatory diet may result in somewhat decreased discomfort from inflammation. Although this diet is not the sole cure, it may help with any therapy.

People who follow an anti-inflammatory diet can absorb antioxidants better in the body. They support the body's capacity to lessen free radicals. What to eat, then, is the question about anti-inflammatory diets that are most questioned. The diversified diet includes a wide range of fruits, whole grains, vegetables, fish, plant-based proteins (nuts and legumes), fatty foods, and a variety of sauces, spices, and dressings. All food must be organic, and that is the sole requirement. The most well-liked anti-inflammatory meals include leafy greens, raspberries, cherries, blackberries, cucumbers, tomatoes, and other berries and vegetables. Choose brown rice, oats, and other high-fiber grains when contemplating whole grains. Herbs and spices are natural antioxidants that might improve your health and food taste. Avoid eating fatty and highly processed foods (such as chocolate, sugary beverages, French fries, ice cream, hamburgers, deli meats, and sausages).

The positive effects of anti-inflammatory therapy are increased by daily consumption of the recommended amounts of water. It's simple to count. To assist you in doing it properly, you may use various tools. The body's cleansing process could be aided by drinking adequate water.

One meal won't be enough to enhance someone's health. It's crucial to eat a variety of nutritious meals. Adding 30 minutes of light exercise each day. Practice good sleep habits since getting too little sleep might go worse.

The most crucial thing to realize before beginning a diet is that it is not a cure-all and only serves to assist the body through a challenging period of therapy. You can start your new, healthy lifestyle with one simple step and see results in less than a year. You may be sure that a transformation in your appearance and increased energy levels will reward your efforts.

The information and advice in this book have been formulated after careful reading and following the Guidelines of HHS.gov U.S. Department of Health & Human Services & U.S. Department of Agriculture. The Center for Nutrition Policy and Promotion (CNPP) develops and promotes the best dietary guidelines for the nutritional needs of Americans based on scientific research and the latest findings from medical science.

CHAPTER 1:
ANTI-INFLAMMATORY DIET

The Major Components of an Anti-Inflammatory Diet are identifiable healthy fats, complex carbohydrates, plenty of fruits and vegetables, legumes, and nutrient-dense meals. Within the best diet you will find, at most once or twice a week, processed meals, refined grains (white bread and white flour), excess added sugars, or red meat, but these foods are not recommended. The human body's response to acute damage is inflammation, but if we are dealing with chronic inflammation, it surely derives from chronic disorders. Numerous disorders, including autoimmune disorders, cancers, chronic renal disease, fatty liver disease, and neurological disorders, are caused by chronic inflammation in the body. Inflammatory problems can be beneficially reduced by maintaining a healthy lifestyle, getting enough sleep, exercising, reducing daily stress, and consuming the right foods that help reduce inflammation. The anti-inflammatory diet is similar to the Mediterranean diet which is very popular because it recommends a healthy diet that can improve the overall health of the body. Both diets recommend eliminating processed nutritious, red meat and foods with added sugar from meals while recommending nutrient-dense meals containing healthy fats and nutrient-rich vegetables. The anti-inflammatory plan advocates eating foods that are proven to reduce inflammation, such as dark green leafy vegetables and red and blue fruits and vegetables, such as cherries, berries, pomegranates, and beets.

Anti-inflammatory foods include:
• Nutrients
• Antioxidants
• Healthful fats

Foods that may aid with inflammation management include:
• fruits; blueberries, strawberries, blackberries, and cherries
• oily fish, tuna, and salmon
• beans
• vegetables, including Avocado, spinach, kale, beets, chard, Cauliflower, and broccoli
• nuts and seeds
• legumes; chickpeas, lentils, and other beans
• fiber
• Sweet Potato
• Citrus Fruit
• Garlic, Herbs, and Spices
• Greek Yogurt & Kefir
• Natural Nut Butter
• Whole Grain; Brown rice, whole wheat bread, and Quinoa
• olives and olive oil

Foods to avoid

No one meal will improve a person's health. The use of a wide range of nutritious foods, especially fresh and unprocessed foods, is recommended in the anti-inflammatory diet. Foods may lose their nutritional value as a result of processing. People should read the labels on prepared meals before eating them. While cocoa is a healthy option, many cocoa-based goods include sugar and fat. If you're on an anti-inflammatory diet, you should avoid or restrict your consumption of the following foods divided according to disorders:

Fatty liver disease
• Alcohol
• Added sugar
• Fried Foods
• Added Salts
• White bread, pasta, and rice
• Red meat

Endometriosis
• Alcohol
• Caffeine
• Fatty meat
• Processed Foods
• Sugary Drinks

Inflammatory bowel disease (IBD)
• Hot/spicy foods.
• Fatty, fried, or greasy foods.
• Raw, high-fiber vegetables & fruits.
• Caffeinated/sugary beverages.
• Nuts, seeds & beans.
• Added sugar.
• Alcoholic beverages.

Asthma
• Dried fruit, i.e., dried cherries and apricots
• Shrimp
• Wine or beer
• Pickles
• Maraschino cherries
• Packaged/prepared potatoes
• Any foods that you're allergic

Rheumatoid arthritis
• Red meat
• Sugar & refined flour
• Fried foods
• Gluten
• Alcohol
• Processed foods

Obesity
• Refined Grains
• Sugary Foods
• Trans Fats & Processed Foods
• Red Meat
• Aerated or Sugary Beverages

Alzheimer's & Parkinson's diseases
• Processed foods
• Foods hard to chew
• High Saturated fat foods

Cancer
• Processed Meat
• Processed Foods
• Alcohol
• Charred Meat
• Sugar-sweetened beverages

CHAPTER 2:
"ITALIAN WAY" INSTRUCTIONS FOR USE

People who reside in Mediterranean Sea-ringed nations, such as Italy and Greece, have historically had a diet high in fruits, vegetables, nuts, seeds, fish, whole grains, & olive oil – the same foods doctors advise to reduce inflammation. Over time, studies showed that those who followed this way of eating experienced lower rates of sickness & lived longer than Americans who maintained a Western-style diet.

Doctors and nutritionists value the Mediterranean diet for a good cause. Some university studies have shown that the anti-inflammatory diet protects against chronic inflammatory disorders such as cardiovascular disease, type 2 diabetes, and metabolic syndrome Additionally, the Mediterranean diet is extremely simple to keep to and maintain since it comprises a range of foods.

By finding a balance between the meals you choose to eat and the things you avoid, the greatest way to get better sleep & better health is to eat various foods. In other words, adopt a balanced eating pattern that centers meals on anti-inflammatory foods and avoids fried, fast, & processed foods if you want to enhance your sleep and lower your risk of chronic illnesses shortly.

Studies emphasized that although the anti-inflammatory properties of a Mediterranean diet are significant, these foods also have additional advantages. Adiponectin, a hormone that controls glucose levels and promotes the fatty acid breakdown and is crucial for healthy sleep cycles as well as lowering the risks of diabetes, heart disease, obesity, and possibly even arthritis and osteoporosis, can be improved by the Mediterranean diet in addition to its anti-inflammatory and anti-oxidative effects.

Your diet may need to be changed if you are caught in a loop of little sleep, bad eating, insufficient exercise, and excessive stress. Without sufficient sleep, the body is more likely to make more of the hormone ghrelin, which tells your brain that you should eat immediately. Leptin, the hormone that signals the brain to slow down eating, is also decreased by sleep deprivation.

On the other hand, insufficient leptin signals the brain to increase food intake. You will probably get better sleep, regulate your digestive hormones, and, most significantly, reduce your general risk of chronic conditions that will likely worsen with age if you follow an eating strategy that resembles the Mediterranean diet.

Special Recommendations: read before you start

A healthy eating pattern is essential at every stage of life, from infancy to adulthood, and it's never too late or too early to start eating healthily. The best way to reduce the risk of chronic inflammatory diseases is to follow a healthy eating pattern to achieve a healthy body, maintain a balanced hormonal system and increase vitality and fertility.

It is very important to follow a personalized diet, which describes within the recommended caloric limits, contains foods and drinks rich in nutrients, reflects personal preferences and territorial and cultural traditions, and is in line with one's budget.

The following principles inspire a healthy food model:
1) The nutritional elements must be taken above all from foods and drinks rich in nutrients and which provide vitamins and minerals, remaining low in added sugars, saturated fats, and sodium.

2) Nutritional elements are obtained mainly through vegetables, fruits, lactose-free dairy products or fortified soy beverages, protein foods such as lean meats, poultry and eggs, beans, peas and lentils, nuts and soybeans, vegetable oils

3) Foods with added sugars, saturated fats, sodium, and alcoholic beverages are limited (better if excluded).

4) A healthy daily meal includes nutrients from the above groups within the recommended daily calorie intake.

Federal agencies have collected data over the past 40 years, and it has emerged that Americans generally do not comply with the recommendations of dietary guides published over time, so the levels of chronic inflammatory diseases linked to improper diet, so much so that it has become a major concern for public health.

The main health problems are:
Cardiovascular Diseases (Coronary Heart Disease, Hypertension, High LDL and Total Blood Cholesterol, Stroke), Diabetes, Overweight and Obesity, and Cancer.

Therefore, making a healthy choice and starting a healthy and nutritious food pattern can greatly impact every citizen's quality of life and health. All it takes are small changes and healthy choices, as you will learn by following the food advice in this book and cooking the simple and tasty recipes proposed.

University scientific studies have shown that maintaining a healthy eating pattern consistently reduces the risk of inflammatory and chronic diseases.

Key dietary principles
1) Nutritional needs must be met with food and drink
2) Choose foods from each food group (fruits, vegetables, protein foods)
3) Pay attention to caloric values and portion sizes so as not to exceed the daily requirement

To achieve a healthy dietary model, it is good to start with personal preferences, combining cultural traditions and considering the budget. Even by doing low-cost shopping, it is possible to eat in a healthy and tasty way.

Following the recommendations on food safety and the recipes in this book will help you eat in a healthy and varied way, composing meals that are always tasty and rich in nutrients useful for filling your body with energy.

The basis of a healthy diet is to preserve food healthily and safely, following these four basic principles: clean, separate, cook, and cool.

Get used to a healthy diet and achieve a simple and healthy lifestyle if you eat one meal at a time, one day at a time, until it becomes a pleasant habit. Small changes won't upset your habits, but slowly they will lead you to a healthy and lasting regimen.

To achieve this goal, it is important to combine the main meals (breakfast, lunch, and dinner, with at least two snacks, one in the morning and one in the afternoon), always considering not exceeding the daily calorie requirement.

Reading the values contained in the product labels allows you to make healthy food choices and respect the daily limits.

Finally, the importance of physical activity is recognized by all studies carried out on health because it allows us to be more active, healthier, to have lower risks of chronic diseases than inactive people, allowing us to obtain immediate benefits on mood and sleep as well as stress, as well as having long-term benefits for bone health, reduction of obesity and cardiovascular disease, type 2 diabetes, depression and many types of cancer.

It is advisable to perform a physical activity of at least 150-300 minutes of moderate-intensity aerobic activity, such as a walk fast, every week, also combining simple exercises to strengthen the major muscle groups.

For this reason, we have included a SPECIAL BONUS inside the book containing the best physical exercises to start with and a complete plan to help you find your body's stimuli by quickly and easily reaching your weekly goal.

Federal agency studies and university research show that overweight and obesity affect 74 percent of adults in the United States, significantly increasing their risk of developing other chronic health conditions, including cardiovascular disease, type 2 diabetes, and some cancers.

Inside the book, you will find a 28-day food plan to help you start a healthy eating pattern to reduce the problem of being overweight or obese.

It is important to remember that calorie needs differ between women and men and decrease with age, so men between the ages of 19 and 30 require between 2,400 and 3,000 calories per day, while women require 1,800 to 2,400 calories per day. It is lower for adults aged 31 to 59; males require 2,200 to 3,000 calories per day, while 1,600 to 2,200 calories per day are sufficient for women.

One very healthy habit that this book encourages us is to eat self-prepared meals without buying pre-prepared foods, which turn out to be less healthy and more expensive."

CHAPTER 3:
BREAKFAST RECIPES

FERTILITY-BOOSTING PUDDING PARFAIT

INGREDIENTS

For Chia Seed Pudding Base:
- 1/4 cup of maple syrup
- ½ cup of chia seeds
- 1 can or 1 ½ cup of unsweetened & full-fat coconut milk
- 2 heaping tbsp of almond butter
- ¼ tsp of pink Himalayan Sea salt
- 2 tsp of vanilla extract

For Cherry Compote:
- 1/3 cup of coconut sugar or use maple syrup
- 2 cinnamon sticks
- 2 cups of organic cherries; pitted & chopped

Additional Topping Options:
- An extra drizzle of nut butter
- Shredded coconut or use toasted coconut flakes
- Chopped nuts (hazelnuts, pistachios, almonds, macadamias, and cashews) or use more seeds (hemp, pumpkin, etc.)
- Fresh cherries
- Sugar-free granola topping
- Unsweetened & full-fat coconut yogurt

NUTRITIONAL INFORMATION:

Calories: 325 Kcal | Protein: 8 g | Carbohydrates: 41 g | Fat: 16 g | Fiber: 13 g

Prep. Time:	Total Time:	Servings:	Difficulty Level:
5 min.	2 hrs.	4	Medium

DIRECTIONS

To prepare the chia seed pudding base, add vanilla, maple syrup, almond butter, coconut milk, sea salt and whisk to blend. You may also add any other flavorings you want. Add the chia seeds and mix everything well after combining.

The bowl should be refrigerated so it can cool and solidify. For optimal effects it is recommended to leave it on for the whole night, even if two hours could be enough.

Pitted cherries, cinnamon sticks, and coconut sugar should all be added to a stovetop saucepan and heated on high till boiling while the chia is gelling. Once it starts to bubble, reduce the heat and let it simmer for 10 to 20 minutes until it thickens (it should have the consistency of practical jam).

The cinnamon sticks should be removed and put aside to cool. Scoop out 1/4 to 1/2 cup of the chia mixture when ready to consume, top with cherry compote, and then add any additional toppings.

ANTI-INFLAMMATORY SMOOTHIE

INGREDIENTS

- 1 teaspoon of fresh Turmeric; peeled & grated
- 2 cups of ripe strawberries; chopped & frozen
- 1 teaspoon of fresh ginger; peeled & grated
- ½ cup of orange juice
- 2/3 cup of beet; roasted, chopped & frozen
- 1 cup of unsweetened almond milk

Options for serving:
- Goji berries
- Full-fat coconut milk
- Raw cashews

NUTRITIONAL INFORMATION:

Calories: 326 Kcal | Protein: 8 g | Carbohydrates: 61 g | Fat: 10 g | Fiber: 10 g

Prep. Time:	Total Time:	Servings:	Difficulty Level:
5 min.	50 min.	2	Easy

DIRECTIONS

Cut beets into chunks measuring 1/2", wrapped with foil, then bake for 45 to 50 mins at 400 degrees F. The beet may be cut in half and steamed for 20 minutes or until it yields to a fork prick test. After cooking your beet, let it cool, then put it in the freezer for two hours. Because you may need 2/3 cup, you could have leftover roasted beet that you can use in salads. Blend all the ingredients in a blender until they are perfectly smooth. Serve with goji berries and full-fat coconut milk.

CHAMOMILE AND MAPLE PORRIDGE

INGREDIENTS

- 1 tablespoon of coconut butter
- Scant 1 cup of plant-based milk (cashew milk)
- 1 teaspoon of maple syrup
- 2 teaspoons of dried chamomile flowers
- ½ cup of rolled oats
- 1 tablespoon of flax seeds /chia seeds
- Sliced almonds; toasted (for garnish)

NUTRITIONAL INFORMATION:

Calories: 398 Kcal | Protein: 10 g | Carbohydrates: 46 g | Fat: 21 g | Fiber: 2 g

Prep. Time:	Total Time:	Servings:	Difficulty Level:
5 min.	15 min.	1	Easy

DIRECTIONS

Combine the oats, a scant 1/2 cup (115ml) of boiling water, and the plant-based milk in a sizeable saucepan over low heat. Add chamomile tea leaves or flowers. Cook while stirring continuously for 10 minutes. Remove any bigger flower pieces if desired. Add the almond slices, maple syrup, coconut butter, and flax or chia seeds as garnishes.

MEXICAN BREAKFAST HASH

INGREDIENTS

- 3 Sweet Potatoes; large dice
- 2 tsp of Poultry Seasoning
- 1 Jalapeno Pepper; minced
- 2 Poblano peppers; small dice
- 1 tbsp of Fennel Seed
- 2 tsp of Minced Garlic
- 1 pound of Ground pork
- ½ Red Onion; small dice
- 1 tsp of Cumin
- 2 tsp of Chili Powder
- 2 tbsp of Avocado Oil
- 1 tsp of Smoked Paprika
- ¼ cup of Fresh Cilantro chopped
- Salt/Pepper; to taste
- 1 Lime; wedges

Prep. Time:	Total Time:	Servings:	Difficulty Level:
10 min.	45 min.	4	Easy

DIRECTIONS

Set your oven to 400 degrees F. Sweet potatoes are diced into bite-sized pieces and tossed with 1 tablespoon of oil. Place on a baking sheet and cook in the oven for 30 to 40 minutes, stirring halfway through.

In a big skillet, warm the remaining oil over medium-high heat. Before adding garlic, peppers, onion, and spices sauté the ground pork with the poultry seasoning and fennel for approximately 5 minutes.

Cook the meat and veggies together in a pan until they are tender. Top roasted sweet potatoes with meat mixture, cilantro, and lime.

NUTRITIONAL INFORMATION:

Calories: 518 Kcal | Protein: 32 g | Carbohydrates: 27 g | Fat: 31g | Fiber: 6 g

CHIA PUDDING

INGREDIENTS

- 4 oz Soft Tofu
- 1 cup of blueberries
- 375 ml Almond Milk; Almond Breeze
- 1/4 cup of Sliced Almonds
- 1/2 tsp of Pure Almond Extract
- 1/4 cup of Chia Seeds

Prep. Time:	Total Time:	Servings:	Difficulty Level:
15 min.	45 min.	4	Easy

DIRECTIONS

Combine tofu, almond milk, and extract in a blender (or food processor). Blend until the mixture is smooth and thoroughly blended. Transfer to a bowl, mix in the chia seeds, and set aside for 10 minutes. Heat a small pan over low-medium heat, add the almond slices, and constantly stir until they are gently toasted. Remove the pan from the heat and put it aside. Add blueberries to the chia seed mixture gently. Chia pudding should be refrigerated before serving. Distribute equally among four small dishes; if preferred, top with the toasted almonds and more blueberries.

NUTRITIONAL INFORMATION:

Calories: 187 Kcal | Protein: 9 g | Carbohydrates: 11 g | Fat: 12 g | Fiber: 8 g

HOMEMADE MUESLI

INGREDIENTS

- 1/2 cup of wheat bran
- 3 1/2 cups of rolled oats
- 1/2 teaspoon of ground cinnamon
- 1/2 teaspoon of kosher salt
- 1/4 cup of raw pecans: coarsely chopped
- 1/2 cup of sliced almonds
- 1/2 cup of unsweetened coconut flakes
- 1/4 cup of raw pepitas: (shelled pumpkin seeds)
- 1/4 cup of dried cherries
- 1/4 cup of dried apricots: coarsely chopped

NUTRITIONAL INFORMATION:

Calories: 275 kcal | Protein: 8.5 g | Carbohydrates: 36.4 g | Fat: 13 g | Fiber: 7.5 g

Prep. Time:	Total Time:	Servings:	Difficulty Level:
15 min.	15 min.	8	Medium

DIRECTIONS

Grain, nuts, and seeds are lightly toasted. Heat an oven to 350°F and split it into thirds using two racks. On a rimmed baking sheet, mix the salt, wheat bran, oats, and cinnamon; toss to blend and distribute into an equal layer. On a second rimmed baking sheet, add the almonds, pecans, and pepitas; toss them and distribute them into an equal layer. Place the oats on the top rack and the nuts on the bottom rack in the oven. Bake for 10 to 12 minutes or until nuts are aromatic.

Toss in the coconut. Take the baking sheet with nuts out of the oven and put it aside to cool. Sprinkle the coconut over the oats, return to the top rack, and bake for another 5 minutes or until the coconut is golden brown. Remove them from the oven and put them aside for 10 minutes to cool.

Place them in a large mixing bowl. Add dried fruit to the mix. Toss in the cherries and apricots to combine. Place the contents in an airtight container. Muesli may be kept at room temperature for up to a month in an airtight container.

Enjoy as you want. Serve with fresh fruit and a sprinkle of honey or maple syrup, like overnight oats, oatmeal, cereal, or yogurt.

FRESH TURMERIC SMOOTHIE BOWL

INGREDIENTS

- 1 orange
- 1 cup of frozen mango
- 1/2 lemon
- 1 cup of frozen cauliflower
- 1 tbsp of coconut oil
- 1-inch piece of fresh Turmeric
- 1/2 cup of water / more, depending on the consistency
- pinch of black pepper

Toppings:
- Golden berries
- coconut
- bee pollen
- mango

Prep. Time:	Total Time:	Servings:	Difficulty Level:
5 min.	0 min.	6	Medium

DIRECTIONS

Blend all of the ingredients until they are thick and smooth. Add chosen (optional) toppings to the top.

NUTRITIONAL INFORMATION:

Calories: 24 kcal | protein: 8 g | carbohydrates: 15 g | Fat: 25 g | Fiber: 7 g

SWEET POTATO TOASTS

INGREDIENTS

- ¼ cup of peanut butter/ almond butter
- 1 medium sweet potato; sliced into ¼-inch thick slices
- 1 banana; sliced

Prep. Time:	Total Time:	Servings:	Difficulty Level:
5 min.	5 min.	6	Medium

DIRECTIONS

Cut the sweet potato in half and remove the ends. Make 4 slices by slicing them lengthwise into 1/4-inch-thick pieces. Toast the pieces in a toaster. Toast for 2-3 minutes on high or until nicely browned on the outside and cooked through on the inside. Rep with the remaining two slices. Using 1 tablespoon of desired butter, spread 1 tablespoon on each slice. Close the sandwiches by adding banana slices on top.

NUTRITIONAL INFORMATION:

Calories: 151 kcal | Protein: 4.4 g | Carbohydrates: 16.9 g | Fat: 8.4 g | Fiber: 2.5 g

SOUTHWEST TOFU SCRAMBLE

INGREDIENTS

Scramble
- 1-2 Tbsp of avocado oil/olive oil
- 8 of extra-firm tofu
- ¼ thinly sliced red onion.
- 2 cups of loosely chopped kale.
- 1/2 thinly sliced red pepper.

Sauce
- 1/2 tsp of garlic powder
- 1/2 tsp of sea salt (low quantity for less salty sauce)
- 1/4 tsp of chili powder
- 1/2 tsp of ground cumin
- 1/4 tsp of Turmeric (optional)
- Water (too thin)

For Serving (Optional)
- Cilantro
- Salsa
- Breakfast potatoes, fruit, or toast

NUTRITIONAL INFORMATION:

Calories: 212 Kcal | Protein: 16.4 g | Carbohydrates: 7.1 g | Fat: 15.1 g | Fiber: 3 g

Prep. Time:	Total Time:	Servings:	Difficulty Level:
5 min.	30 min.	2	Easy

DIRECTIONS

Roll tofu in a clean, absorbent cloth for 15 minutes with anything heavy on top, such as a cast-iron pan. Prepare the sauce by combining dry spices in a small dish and adding enough water to create a pourable sauce while the tofu drains. Set it aside.

Heat a wide skillet on medium heat while preparing the vegetables. When the pan is heated, add the onion, red pepper, and olive oil. Stir in salt and pepper to taste. Cook for 5 minutes or until softened. Add the kale, season with a pinch of salt and pepper, and cover for 2 minutes to steam.

Meanwhile, unwrap the tofu and crush it with a fork into bite-sized pieces.

Move the vegetables to one side of the pan and add the tofu using a spatula. After 2 minutes, add the sauce and pour it mainly over the tofu and a little over the vegetables. Stir quickly to distribute the sauce evenly. Cook for 5-7 minutes or until the tofu has browned slightly. Serve with toast, breakfast potatoes, or fruit. Spicy sauce, salsa, and fresh cilantro are the favorite ways to ramp up the taste.

BABY KALE BREAKFAST SALAD WITH QUINOA & STRAWBERRIES

INGREDIENTS

- 2 teaspoons of apple cider vinegar
- 1 tablespoon of extra-virgin olive oil
- 3 cups of lightly packed baby kale
- 1 teaspoon of minced garlic
- Pinch of ground pepper
- ½ cup of cooked quinoa
- 1 tablespoon of salted pepitas
- Pinch of salt
- ½ cup of sliced strawberries

NUTRITIONAL INFORMATION:

Calories: 330 Kcal | Protein: 9g | Carbohydrates: 31 g | Fat: 20.1 g | Fiber: 5.9 g

Prep. Time:	Total Time:	Servings:	Difficulty Level:
15 min.	15 min.	1	Easy

DIRECTIONS

To make a paste, mash the garlic and salt with a fork or a chef's knife. Mix the oil, garlic paste, vinegar, and pepper in a medium bowl. Stir in the kale and toss to coat. Serve with strawberries, quinoa, and pepitas on the side.

PARSLEY FRITTATA

INGREDIENTS

- 6 beaten eggs,
- ¼ cup of plain yogurt
- ½ cup of chopped parsley,
- ½ teaspoon of cayenne pepper
- 1 teaspoon of olive oil

NUTRITIONAL INFORMATION:

Calories: 119 Kcal | Protein: 9.4 g | Carbohydrates: 2.2 g | Fat: 8 g | Fiber: 0.3 g

Prep. Time:	Total Time:	Servings:	Difficulty Level:
10 min.	30 min.	4	Medium

DIRECTIONS

Combine parsley, eggs, plain yogurt, and cayenne pepper in a mixing bowl. After that, pour olive oil into the pan and heat it thoroughly. Pour an egg mixture into the skillet, carefully flatten it, and cover it. Cook the frittata for 20 minutes over medium heat.

OATMEAL WITH TURMERIC POWDER

INGREDIENTS

• 1 teaspoon turmeric powder
• 1 cup whole oats, rolled
• 2 milk splashes
• 2 cups water

NUTRITIONAL INFORMATION:

Calories: 154.6 Kcal | Protein: 5.1 g |
Carbohydrates: 29.2 g | Fat: 3.1 g | Fiber: 12 g

Prep. Time:	Total Time:	Servings:	Difficulty Level:
5 min.	20 min.	2	Easy

DIRECTIONS

In 2 cups of boiling water, add your oats. Cook for about 10 minutes with the heat reduced to medium, stirring often. About minute five, add your splashes of milk with the teaspoon of turmeric powder, and keep stirring.

When the oatmeal is done cooking, spoon it into a bowl and top it with your choice of toppings. You may eat it plain as well. Whatever the case, this oatmeal is both wholesome and tasty.

ZUCCHINI OATMEAL

INGREDIENTS

• 1 Cup of Zucchini; Shredded
• 1/3 Cup of Oatmeal
• 1 Tbsp of Stevia
• 1 Cup of Unsweetened Almond Milk
• 1/4 Tsp of Nutmeg
• 1 Tsp of Cinnamon
• 1 Tsp of Vanilla Extract
• Dash of Sea Salt
• 1 Tbsp of Pecans; Chopped
• 1 Tbsp of Raisins

Prep. Time:	Total Time:	Servings:	Difficulty Level:
10 min.	15 min.	1	Easy

DIRECTIONS

Boil the milk in a saucepan on the stove, adding all ingredients except the raisins and pecans. Reduce to low heat and cook until most of the liquid has almost been absorbed. Pour into a bowl and top with raisins and pecans when done. Note: You can prepare this up to 4 days ahead of time and keep it in the fridge, then reheat and add toppings when ready to eat.

NUTRITIONAL INFORMATION:

Calories: 226 kcal | Protein: 7 g | Carbohydrates: 34 g | Fat: 9 g | Fiber: 7 g

APPLE-CINNAMON OVERNIGHT OATS

INGREDIENTS

- ¼ teaspoon of ground cinnamon
- 1 teaspoon of maple syrup
- ½ cup of unsweetened almond milk
- Pinch of salt
- ½ tablespoon of chia seeds (Optional)
- ½ cup of old-fashioned Gluten-free rolled oats.
- 2 tablespoons of toasted pecans (Optional)
- ½ cup of diced apple

NUTRITIONAL INFORMATION:

Calories: 215 Kcal | Protein: 5.7 g | Carbohydrates: 40.8 g | fat; 4.4 g | Fiber: 6.3 g

Prep. Time:	Total Time:	Servings:	Difficulty Level:
10 min.	6 hrs.	1	Easy

DIRECTIONS

Mix the almond milk, oats, cinnamon, chia seeds, maple syrup, and salt in a pint-sized jar. Refrigerate overnight after covering it. If desired, garnish with pecans and apple before serving.

SPANISH OMELET

INGREDIENTS

- 1 medium chopped onion,
- 3 large eggs
- ½ tsp of coconut oil
- 200g potatoes

NUTRITIONAL INFORMATION:

Calories: 482 Kcal | Protein: 29 g | Carbohydrates: 47 g | Fat: 17.4 g | Fiber: 7.3 g

Prep. Time:	Total Time:	Servings:	Difficulty Level:
30 min.	40 min.	2	Easy

DIRECTIONS

Peel and finely slice the potatoes. Spread the slices on one side of the tea towel, then drape the half without the slices over the top. To eliminate any extra liquid, press down on them. Add the coconut oil to a deep-frying pan, heat it over medium/high heat, and add potatoes and onions. Cover and simmer for 20 minutes, stirring regularly.

In a mixing dish, whisk together the eggs, add the cooked onions and potatoes, and stir well. Return everything to the frying pan and cook over medium heat, covered, until the egg is set.

Place a big plate over the frying pan, flip it upside down, so the omelet flows out, and then slide it back into the pan. Cook for another 5 minutes before serving.

Chapter 4:
Appetizer Recipes

SWEET POTATO SOUP

INGREDIENTS

- 1 cubed white onion,
- 4 tablespoons of extra virgin olive oil
- 1 chopped garlic clove,
- pinch of cinnamon
- 1 teaspoon of black pepper; fresh, cracked
- 3/4 tablespoon of salt
- 1 tablespoon of sweet yellow curry powder
- pinch of cloves
- 1 teaspoon of cayenne pepper
- 3 medium-sized cubed sweet potatoes,
- 1 teaspoon of turmeric
- 4 cups of hot water
- 1 liter of vegetable stock; low-sodium
- 2 medium-sized cubed white potatoes,
- 1 13.66-ounce can of lite coconut milk
- 1 large zucchini; width-wise

NUTRITIONAL INFORMATION:

Calories: 180 Kcal | Protein: 2 g | Carbohydrates: 21 g | Fat: 10 g | Fiber: 4.1 g

Prep. Time:	Total Time:	Servings:	Difficulty Level:
1 hr.	1 hr. 10 min.	8	Easy

DIRECTIONS

Clean, chop, and cube all of your veggies. Put it aside. Add 4 tablespoons of extra virgin olive oil to a big saucepan. Add onion and allow it to cook for a few minutes. Allow it to sweat for 5 mins on low heat.

Season with pepper, salt, and garlic. Stir it well before adding the potatoes. Add potatoes and allow for a 5-minute cook time on medium heat to get brown color. To prevent burning, keep stirring.

Toss in the stalk and a splash of water. Bring to a boil, reduce to low heat, and cook for 20-25 minutes. Add zucchini halfway through the cooking process. Add coconut milk after 20-25 minutes. Do a fork text before putting the soup in the blender to ensure the potatoes are cooked.

Purée the soup in a blender. Garnish with lemon juice, black pepper, and herbs and spices.

TOMATO & GREENS SALAD

INGREDIENTS

- ½ tablespoon of fresh lemon juice
- 3 cups of fresh baby greens
- 1 tablespoon of olive oil (extra-virgin)
- 1 -1/2 cups of cherry tomatoes

NUTRITIONAL INFORMATION:

Calories: 90 Kcal | Protein: 1.7 g | Carbohydrates: 6.3 g | Fat: 7.3 g | Fiber: 2.2 g

Prep. Time:	Total Time:	Servings:	Difficulty Level:
5 min.	10 min.	2	Easy

DIRECTIONS

Combine all ingredients in a wide mixing bowl and toss well to combine. Serve it.

BROCCOLI WITH GARLIC AND LEMON

INGREDIENTS

- 1 teaspoon of olive oil
- 4 cups of broccoli florets
- 1/4 teaspoon of ground black pepper
- 1 tablespoon of minced garlic
- 1/4 teaspoon of kosher salt
- 1 teaspoon of lemon zest

NUTRITIONAL INFORMATION:

Calories: 45 kcal | Protein: 3 g | carbohydrates: 7 g | Fat: 1 g | Fiber: 3 g

Prep. Time:	Total Time:	Servings:	Difficulty Level:
5 min.	10 min.	4	Medium

DIRECTIONS

Boil one cup of water in a small saucepan. Add broccoli and cook in boiling water for 2 to 3 minutes or until the broccoli is tender. Drain the broccoli and set it aside.

Heat the oil in a small sauté pan over medium-high heat. Sauté garlic for 30 seconds. Add salt, lemon zest, broccoli, and pepper. Toss it well and serve it.

QUINOA AND VEGETABLE SOUP

INGREDIENTS

- 1 chopped onion,
- 2 tablespoons of butter
- ½ cup of diced carrot
- 1 minced clove of garlic,
- 2 tablespoons of dried parsley
- ½ cup of chopped celery
- 1 bay leaf
- 1 teaspoon of dried basil
- 2 tablespoons of olive oil
- 1 pinch of dried thyme
- 2 (32 ounces) cartons of chicken broth
- 2 cups of shredded cabbage
- 1 (28-ounce) can have crushed tomatoes
- ½ cup of grated Parmesan cheese
- 1 (15 ounces) can have drained light red kidney beans,
- ½ cup of quinoa

NUTRITIONAL INFORMATION:

Calories: 280 Kcal | Protein: 11.6 g | Carbohydrates: 31.8 g | Fat: 12.4 g | Fiber: 8.5 g

Prep. Time:	Total Time:	Servings:	Difficulty Level:
30 min.	1 hr. 15 min.	6	Easy

DIRECTIONS

In a wide pot or Dutch oven, heat olive oil and butter over medium heat; sauté and stir the onion, garlic, carrot, and celery until softened, for 5 to 10 minutes. Bring the parsley, basil, thyme, chicken broth, bay leaf, and tomatoes to a boil. Reduce heat to low and cook for 10 minutes or until well heated.

Add kidney beans, cabbage, and quinoa. Cover and cook for 30 minutes or until the quinoa is cooked. Serve with a sprinkling of Parmesan cheese on top of each dish.

BEET HUMMUS

INGREDIENTS

- ⅓ cup of extra-virgin olive oil
- 4 cups of canned chickpeas; drained and rinsed
- 1 medium beet; cooked, peeled & chopped
- 3 tablespoons of tahini
- ¼ cup of fresh lemon juice
- 1 garlic clove; smashed
- Pita chips, crackers, tortilla chips, or chopped vegetables, as desired, for dipping
- Kosher salt & freshly ground black pepper

Prep. Time:	Total Time:	Servings:	Difficulty Level:
15 min.	0 min.	8	Medium

DIRECTIONS

Combine the olive oil, chickpeas, beet, tahini, lemon juice, and garlic in the bowl of a food processor. Season with salt and pepper after pureeing until smooth. Serve with crackers, chips, and vegetables of your choice.

NUTRITIONAL INFORMATION:

Calories: 224 kcal | Protein: 7 g | Carbohydrates: 20 g | Fat: 14 g | Fiber: 1.8 g

ASPARAGUS & SNAP PEA SALAD WITH CRISPY PROSCIUTTO

INGREDIENTS

- 4 slices of prosciutto
- ⅓ cup of slivered almonds
- 1-pound trimmed asparagus; 2-inch pieces
- 2 tablespoons of olive oil; extra-virgin
- ½ teaspoon of fine kosher / sea salt
- 2 tablespoons of balsamic vinegar
- ½ pound of snap peas; 1-inch pieces
- 2 tablespoons of minced shallot
- 1 cup of micro radish greens
- ¼ teaspoon of black pepper; freshly ground.

Prep. Time:	Total Time:	Servings:	Difficulty Level:
5 min.	15 min.	4	Easy

DIRECTIONS

Add the asparagus to a large saucepan of salted water and bring it to a boil. Cook for 1-2 minutes or until the asparagus is slightly soft and bright green. Transfer the asparagus to an ice bath using a slotted spoon. Drain when it has cooled.

Meanwhile, cook the prosciutto in a wide pan over medium heat. Cook for 5-6 minutes, stirring often until the prosciutto is golden and crispy. Cut prosciutto into tiny pieces after draining on a paper towel-lined dish.

In a large mixing bowl, combine the balsamic vinegar, olive oil, salt, shallot, and pepper. Toss in the snap peas, asparagus, and microgreens until evenly coated. Serve with prosciutto slices and almonds on top.

NUTRITIONAL INFORMATION:

Calories: 206 Kcal | Protein: 7 g | Carbohydrates: 13 g | Fat: 14 g | Fiber: 5 g

OATMEAL CRACKERS

INGREDIENTS

- 1/2 teaspoon of garlic powder
- 5/8 cup of flour blend; gluten-free
- 1 1/2 Tablespoons of melted vegan buttery spread.
- 1/4 teaspoon of salt
- 1/2 teaspoon of agave nectar or honey
- a large flake of sea salt; for sprinkling
- 1/2 cup of old-fashioned oats; gluten-free
- 1/4-1/2 cup of water

NUTRITIONAL INFORMATION:

Calories: 135 Kcal | Protein: 3 g | Carbohydrates: 21 g | Fat: 4 g | Fiber: 2 g

Prep. Time:	Total Time:	Servings:	Difficulty Level:
10 min.	26 min.	4	Medium

DIRECTIONS

Preheat the oven to 400 degrees Fahrenheit. In a food processor, grind the gluten-free oats until they form a fine flour. Mix the oat flour, garlic powder, gluten-free flour, and salt in a mixing bowl.

Add 1/4 cup of water, agave or honey, buttery spread, and stir it well. More water should be drizzled, stirring until the dough forms a ball. The dough mustn't be overly moist. Put the dough on a parchment paper-lined baking sheet and cover it with waxed paper. Roll out the dough until it is very thin, approximately 1/8 inch thick. Roll the dough out as evenly as you can.

Remove the waxed paper and put the dough on the cookie sheet's parchment paper. Use a knife to cut the dough into squares, but do not separate them. Pour a little amount of water over the dough and smooth it up.

Top with a sprinkling of sea salt flakes. Bake for 13-16 minutes at 400 degrees, turning the baking sheet once throughout the baking time, until golden brown and crisp. Allow it to cool completely before cutting it into squares.

GRILLED EGGPLANT PROVOLONE

INGREDIENTS

- ¼ teaspoon of dried oregano
- 3 tablespoons of olive oil
- ½ teaspoon of kosher salt
- Four small eggplants, half lengthwise
- 1½ tablespoons of balsamic vinegar
- Black pepper; freshly ground.
- Grilled Salsa
- ½ pound of mild provolone; thick-sliced.

NUTRITIONAL INFORMATION:

Calories: 196 Kcal | Protein: 9 g | Carbohydrates: 13 g | Fat: 13 g | Fiber: 7 g

Prep. Time:	Total Time:	Servings:	Difficulty Level:
30 min.	45 min.	8	Medium

DIRECTIONS

Brush the sliced sides of the eggplants with a mixture of oil, vinegar, and oregano. Season to taste with pepper and salt. Preheat the gas grill to high; after 15 minutes, reduce the heat to medium. (If using charcoal, cook until the coals are completely coated with grey ash.) Grill eggplants cut-side down for approximately 5 minutes or until browned. Top each half of the eggplant with a piece of provolone. For 3 minutes longer, grill them or until the cheese is bubbling. Serve with a side of Grilled Salsa.

MIXED FRUIT SALAD

INGREDIENTS

- 1 Kiwi Fruit
- 1/2 cup small Apples (approx. 4 per lb.)
- 1/2 cup of Raspberries
- 1/2 medium Bananas

NUTRITIONAL INFORMATION:

Calories: 79.2 kcal | Protein: 1.2 g | Carbohydrates: 31.8 g | Fat: 0.5 g | Fiber: 4.5 g

Prep. Time:	Total Time:	Servings:	Difficulty Level:
5 min.	10 min.	2	Medium

DIRECTIONS

Combine bananas, apples, raspberries, and kiwi in a bowl and serve it.

VEGAN KIMCHI

INGREDIENTS

- 4 stalks of green onions, only the green part, pieces
- 1 head napa cabbage; (1 lb.)
- 3 tbsp of red pepper flakes
- 4 cloves garlic; minced
- ½ cup of onions; thinly sliced
- 1-inch ginger; grated
- 2 tbsp of sea salt
- 1 tsp of sugar

NUTRITIONAL INFORMATION:

Calories: 160 kcal | Protein: 6 g | Carbohydrates: 11 g | Fat: 0.5 g | Fiber: 4 g

Prep. Time:	Total Time:	Servings:	Difficulty Level:
20 min.	0 min.	64	Medium

DIRECTIONS

Cabbage is cut in 8 wedges vertically. Slices are placed in a big bowl. After 3–4 minutes, add 2 tablespoons of salt and massage it into the cabbage until it is moist and wilts. For 50 minutes, set it aside. Prepare the remaining ingredients in the meantime. Slice 1/2 cup of onions thinly. The green parts of onions are chopped into 2-inch chunks. Garlic cloves are minced. Fresh ginger is grated. Ginger and garlic are combined into a paste by adding 1 tsp sugar. After 50 minutes, put the cabbage into a colander and give it a good one-minute rinse under cold running water. For 30 minutes, drain the cabbage.

Add the chopped cabbage, green onion pieces, garlic ginger paste, sliced onions, and 3 tbsp. of red pepper flakes into a large bowl. Mix well until combined. Fill clean jars with the mixture, leaving 1 inch of space at the top for fermentation. Place in the refrigerator for up to months for storage after three days on the counter at room temperature. In the refrigerator, fermentation will continue to occur. After three days, the kimchi's top may seem frothy or include tiny bubbles, which indicates fermentation. Kimchi should be thrown out if it smells bad or appears slimy.

GRILLED TOMATOES

INGREDIENTS

• 2 ripe tomatoes, halved vertically
• Olive oil
• Kosher salt

NUTRITIONAL INFORMATION:

Calories: 43 kcal | Protein: 1 g | Carbohydrates: 6 g | Fat: 2 g | Fiber: 2 g

Prep. Time:	Total Time:	Servings:	Difficulty Level:
5 min.	15 min.	2-4	Medium

DIRECTIONS

Cut fresh tomatoes vertically in half, rub them with a little salt and olive oil, and then grill them.

BEET SALAD

INGREDIENTS

• 2-3 ounces of Stilton or blue cheese
• 4, beets (peeled, roasted, chilled, and diced)
• 1/4 cup of fresh basil chopped fine.
• 1/2 cup of pecans or walnuts
• 1/2 cup of fruit or herb vinegar
• Lettuce leaf :1 per person
• 2 tablespoons of olive oil

NUTRITIONAL INFORMATION:

Calories: 283 kcal | Protein: 6 g | Carbohydrates: 16 g | Fat: 16 g | Fiber: 3.8 g

Prep. Time:	Total Time:	Servings:	Difficulty Level:
10 min.	55 min.	4	Easy

DIRECTIONS

Heat the oven to 400°F. Bake beets until soft for 45 mins and cool, peel, and slice them. In a saucepan, add the sugar, water, and nuts. Heat the mixture, stirring continuously until most liquid bubbles are absorbed. Place nuts on aluminum foil until coated and the frying pan is dry. Let it cool, and it can be kept for many months at room temperature. Put up a lettuce bed. Toss the vinegar, basil, and oil with the beets. Spread it on a lettuce bed. Sprinkle nuts and cheese cubes over it. Serve.

WINTER ORANGE & FENNEL SALAD

INGREDIENTS

- 1 large Sicilian orange
- 1/2 bulb fennel
- fine sea salt
- Black pepper, freshly cracked
- fresh Sicilian olive oil

NUTRITIONAL INFORMATION:

Calories: 198 kcal | Protein: 4 g | Carbohydrates: 30 g | Fat: 9 g | Fiber: 7 g

Prep. Time:	Total Time:	Servings:	Difficulty Level:
5 min.	10 min.	4	Easy

DIRECTIONS

Peel the fennel into wedges. Slice an orange horizontally after removing all skin, including the white, using a sharp knife. Slice the fennel very thin. Combine in a bowl with fresh olive oil, pepper, and a dash of fine sea salt.

PARSLEY SAUCE

INGREDIENTS

- 1/4 cup of Ligurian olive oil
- 1 clove of garlic
- bunch of parsley
- 1 lemon zest
- Salt and pepper; to taste
- 1 small hot pepper

NUTRITIONAL INFORMATION:

Calories: 103 kcal | Protein: 3 g | Carbohydrates: 7 g | Fat: 7 g | Fiber: 1 g

Prep. Time:	Total Time:	Servings:	Difficulty Level:
5 min.	5 min.	4	Easy

DIRECTIONS

Blend all ingredients in the processor and enjoy.

CELERY ROOT SALAD

INGREDIENTS

- parsley
- 1/2 head of red cabbage; sliced horizontally.
- 1 lemon juiced
- 1/2 celery root; sliced thin
- salt & paprika; to taste

NUTRITIONAL INFORMATION:

Calories: 66 kcal | protein: 2.3 g | carbohydrates: 14.4 g | Fat: 0.5 g | Fiber: 2.8 g

Prep. Time:	Total Time:	Servings:	Difficulty Level:
5 min.	5 min.	4	Easy

DIRECTIONS

Mix all ingredients in a medium bowl, stir, and serve.

Chapter 5:
First Courses
Meat Recipes

TURMERIC LIME CHICKEN

INGREDIENTS

• 4 halved juicy limes,
• 6 boneless skinless chicken breasts
• 2 cups of Japanese Panko/ (breadcrumbs)
• 3 minced garlic cloves,
• Salt and pepper; to taste.
• 1 Tbsp of turmeric
• 2 Tbsp of cilantro
• 4-5 Tbsp of vegetable oil
• 2 large lightly beaten eggs

NUTRITIONAL INFORMATION:

Calories: 326 Kcal | Protein: 29 g | Carbohydrates: 20 g | Fat: 14 g | Fiber: 2 g

Prep. Time:	Total Time:	Servings:	Difficulty Level:
50 min.	10 min.	6	Medium

DIRECTIONS

Make four small incisions in the middle of each chicken breast and season both sides with salt and pepper. This will enable the marinade taste to permeate the flesh more quickly and consistently, allowing chicken breasts to cook more evenly and faster.

Then, combine minced garlic, fresh lime juice, and chopped cilantro, and add the chicken breasts to the marinade in a large mixing bowl. Allow standing for 30 mins at room temperature after covering the bowl.

In a mixing dish, whisk the eggs using a fork. Combine the panko (or breadcrumbs) and turmeric powder in a separate bowl.

Turn chicken breast into a beaten egg dish to coat it well. Then, using the turmeric/ breadcrumb mixture, cover all sides of each chicken breast.

Cook the chicken breasts in half the quantity of vegetable oil in a large nonstick pan over medium heat for 6-10 minutes on each side. Wipe the pan with a paper towel between batches if required to prevent burnt breadcrumbs. To prevent overloading the pan, decrease the temperature and cook in batches.

Place the chicken on a wide dish lined with double paper towels to absorb some of the oil after it's cooked through (no hint of pink). Serve with fresh mango salsa and your choice of roasted or steamed veggies or in a sandwich.

CHICKEN, AVOCADO & QUINOA BOWLS WITH HERB DRESSING

INGREDIENTS

- 5 skinless, boneless chicken thighs (1 1/4 pounds); trimmed.
- Roasted Chicken Thighs
- ¼ teaspoon of salt
- ½ teaspoon of ground pepper

Quinoa
- 1 tablespoon of olive oil; extra-virgin
- 3 cups of chicken broth; low-sodium
- 1½ cups of quinoa
- ¼ teaspoon of salt

Italian Dressing
- 5 tablespoons of water
- ¾ cup of red wine vinegar
- 2 teaspoons of dried oregano
- 1 large clove of garlic
- 2 teaspoons of dried basil
- 1½ tablespoons of sugar
- ½ teaspoon of salt
- 1 tablespoon of Dijon mustard
- 1¾ cups of olive oil; extra-virgin
- ½ teaspoon of ground pepper

Toppings
- 1 sliced avocado,
- 1 (15-ounce) can of chickpeas; rinsed
- 6 thinly sliced radishes,
- ¼ cup of toasted seeds/chopped nuts.
- 1 cup of sprouts or shoots

NUTRITIONAL INFORMATION:

Calories: 753 Kcal | Protein: 34.4 g |
Carbohydrates: 43.3 g | Fat: 50 g | Fiber: 10.3 g

Prep. Time:	Total Time:	Servings:	Difficulty Level:
15 min.	30 min.	4	Medium

DIRECTIONS

Preheat the oven to 425 degrees Fahrenheit. Place the chicken on the baking pan. Sprinkle 1/4 teaspoon of salt and 1/2 teaspoon of ground pepper to taste. Roast the chicken for 14 to 16 minutes or until the instant-read thermometer in the thickest portion registers 165 degrees F. Cut 4 thighs.

In a large pot, combine 1 tablespoon of oil, broth, and 1/4 teaspoon salt. Bring to a boil over high heat, then reduce to low heat and stir in the quinoa. Reduce heat to low and cook for 15 to 20 minutes until the quinoa has absorbed all liquid and the grains have burst. Take the pan off the heat, cover it, and set it aside for 5 minutes. (Set aside 2 cups for later.) To make the dressing in a blender, combine the water, vinegar, sugar, mustard, basil, garlic, salt, oregano, and pepper. Puree until completely smooth. Slowly drizzle in the oil and purée until the mixture is creamy. (Refrigerate 1 3/4 cups in a big mason jar for up to one week.)

To make the bowls: Distribute 3 cups of quinoa into 4 big shallow dishes. Put chickpeas, radishes, chicken, avocado, and sprouts in it. Sprinkle seeds on it. Drizzle 3/4 cup of dressing on top.

WHITE BEAN AND CHICKEN CHILI BLANCA

INGREDIENTS

- 2 tablespoons of olive oil; extra-virgin
- 1 pound of chicken tenders / skinless, boneless chicken breasts
- 2 garlic cloves
- 1 medium diced onion,
- 2 tablespoons of chopped fresh cilantro,
- 1 cup of corn kernels, fresh or frozen, thawed.
- 2 15-ounce cans of white beans; drained and rinsed.
- 2 teaspoons of ground cumin
- 2 cups of Monterey Jack cheese, grated.
- 1 4-ounce can of chopped green chiles.
- 2 teaspoons of pure chili powder
- 3 cups of water
- 1/8 teaspoon of cayenne pepper

NUTRITIONAL INFORMATION:

Calories: 180.3 Kcal | Protein: 15 g | Carbohydrates: 16 g | Fat: 6 g | Fiber: 1 g

Prep. Time:	Total Time:	Servings:	Difficulty Level:
20 min.	1hr. 20 min.	8	Medium

DIRECTIONS

Using salt and pepper, season the chicken. Heat oil in a large skillet over high heat, add the chicken pieces, cook it, and occasionally turn until browned; it will take about 2-3 minutes. Reduce the heat to medium-low and add the onion and garlic. Cook for 5-6 minutes or until the onion is transparent. Add chiles, beans, spices, corn, and water. Bring to a boil, lower to low heat, and let simmer for 1 hour, uncovered. Add a tablespoon of cheese and a sprinkle of cilantro to each serving.

PULLED PORK

INGREDIENTS

- 2 teaspoons of sumac
- 1 tablespoon of dark brown sugar
- 2kg pork shoulder (joint or steaks)
- 3 tablespoons of apple cider vinegar
- 2 teaspoons of garlic salt
- 2 tablespoons of black treacle or molasses
- 150 ml apple juice

To serve
- Slices of fresh apple
- Gluten freerolls
- Apple sauce
- white and red cabbage; Shredded

NUTRITIONAL INFORMATION:

Calories: 254 Kcal | Protein: 15 g | Carbohydrates: 16 g | Fat: 14 g | Fiber: 2 g

Prep. Time:	Total Time:	Servings:	Difficulty Level:
10 min.	8-10 hrs. slow cooker cooking	4	Medium

DIRECTIONS

Sumac, garlic salt/salt, and dark brown sugar are rubbed into the pork. Place it in a slow cooker or a big saucepan with a cover. Pour the vinegar, apple juice, and treacle/molasses over the meat. Cover and cook on Low for 8-10 hours in a slow cooker or 2 hours per kilogram in a normal oven at 140C/120 Fan. Shoulder steaks cook faster than joint steaks. Take the pork out of the fluids after it has finished cooking. Using two forks, shred the meat. To remove the fat, strain the liquid and chill it. Reheat the pork with the drained liquids before serving it with your favorite toppings on a bun.

ROASTED CHICKEN WITH BALSAMIC VINAIGRETTE

INGREDIENTS

- 2 tablespoons of Dijon mustard
- 1 teaspoon of lemon zest
- 2 tablespoons of fresh lemon juice
- 1/4 cup of balsamic vinegar
- 2 chopped garlic cloves,
- Salt
- 2 tablespoons of olive oil
- 1 (4-pound) whole chicken; sliced
- black pepper; Freshly ground.
- 1/2 cup of chicken broth; low-salt
- 1 tablespoon of fresh parsley leaves; chopped.

NUTRITIONAL INFORMATION:

Calories: 189.9 Kcal | Protein: 24.4 g | Carbohydrates: 8.1 g | Fat: 7.3 g | Fiber: 2 g

Prep. Time:	Total Time:	Servings:	Difficulty Level:
20 min.	1 hr. (plus 2 to 24 hours for chicken to marinate)	4	Medium

DIRECTIONS

Whisk together the mustard, lemon juice, vinegar, olive oil, salt, garlic, and pepper in a small bowl. In a wide resealable plastic bag, combine the chicken pieces and vinaigrette; close the bag and toss them to coat. Refrigerate for about 2 hours and up to one day, rotating the chicken pieces periodically.

Preheat oven to 400 degrees Fahrenheit. Remove the chicken from the bag and place it in a large baking dish that has been sprayed. Roast for 1 hour or until chicken is cooked through. Cover the chicken with foil for the cooking time if it browns too fast. Place the chicken on a serving dish and serve.

Place the baking dish on a low-medium heat stove. Scrape up any browned pieces on the bottom of a baking sheet with a wooden spoon and whisk them into the broth and pan drippings. Drizzle the chicken with the pan drippings. Serve the chicken with parsley and lemon zest.

SWEET & SOUR CHICKEN

INGREDIENTS

- 1 tbsp of tomato puree
- 1/2 cube of chicken stock
- 6 tbsp of apple juice /pineapple juice
- 1 tbsp of rice wine /sherry
- 1 tsp of coconut oil/vegetable oil
- 1 tbsp of rice vinegar /white wine vinegar
- 1 tbsp of corn flour
- 1 clove of garlic
- 400 g chicken breast
- 1 tsp of fresh ginger; grated.
- 1 whole green pepper
- 1 spring onion
- 1 whole red pepper
- 150 g fresh pineapple/ 2 rings of tinned pineapple
- 1 medium onion

NUTRITIONAL INFORMATION:

Calories: 290.6 Kcal | Protein: 8 g | Carbohydrates: 52 g | Fat: 5 g | Fiber: 1 g

Prep. Time:	Total Time:	Servings:	Difficulty Level:
20 min.	30 min.	3	Easy

DIRECTIONS

For sauce making, combine 1/2 stock cube with the 2 tbsp of boiling water in a heat-proof dish and stir until dissolved. Add vinegar, apple/pineapple juice, rice wine, tomato puree, and corn flour. Stir well and set aside. Cut onions, peppers, and pineapple into 2 cm pieces and set aside. Reserve the chicken breast, which should be chopped into the same size cubes as the veggies. Garlic and ginger should be coarsely grated or crushed, and spring onions should be neatly sliced. Heat the oil in a wok or heavy-bottomed pan over high heat.

Add ginger, garlic, and spring onion, then the chicken. Stir-fry chicken for 5-6 mins over high heat, stirring continuously, until it is fully done. If necessary, add a tbsp. of water at a time. Stir in the onions and peppers for a further 2 minutes. Remove from heat and whisk in the pineapple and sauce until the sauce has thickened and is boiling. Serve with rice or gluten-free noodles.

TURKEY SHEPHERD'S PIE.

INGREDIENTS

- 2 teaspoons of olive oil
- 1.5 pounds of ground turkey
- 3 Tablespoons of ketchup
- 1 chopped onion
- 1 cup of white button-sliced mushrooms.
- 2 minced cloves of garlic
- 1 cup of frozen peas
- 3/4 cup of non-dairy milk
- 1/8 teaspoon of white pepper
- 3 Tablespoons of buttery vegan spread
- 6 peeled gold potatoes; large chunks
- 1/2 teaspoon of salt
- 3/4 cup of cheddar cheese; non-dairy
- 1/2 cup of non-dairy milk

NUTRITIONAL INFORMATION:

Calories: 384 Kcal | Protein: 35 g | Carbohydrates: 34 g | Fat: 12 g | Fiber: 6 g

Prep. Time:	Total Time:	Servings:	Difficulty Level:
15 min.	35 min.	6	Medium

DIRECTIONS

Turn the broiler into a large skillet, and heat olive oil over medium heat. Add mushrooms, garlic, chopped onion, and turkey. Cook until the turkey is fully done. The grease should be removed. Boil the potatoes in a separate pan for approximately 20 minutes while the turkey is cooking. Drain the water, add salt, vegan butter, and ½ cup of milk, and mash the potato with a potato masher.

Toss the ground turkey with pepper, ketchup, and 3/4 cup of non-dairy milk. Stir constantly over low heat until the sauce has thickened somewhat. Stir in the peas until they are well cooked.

Fill a casserole dish halfway with the turkey mixture. Distribute evenly. Spread the mashed potatoes over the turkey and spread them out evenly. Cheese is sprinkled on top. Cover the casserole dish with foil and broil for 5 minutes or until the cheese is browned and melted.

CHEESY BROCCOLI CHICKEN RICE

INGREDIENTS

- 1 chopped onion
- 1 1/2 pounds of chicken breasts; large chunks
- 1 coarsely chopped clove of garlic.
- 32 ounces of chicken broth
- 1 cup of long-grain rice; brown or white; uncooked
- 1/3 teaspoon of pepper
- 1 1/4 teaspoons of salt
- 1 Tablespoon of olive oil
- 1 1/4 cups of cheddar cheese; dairy-free
- 2 cups of broccoli, chopped.

NUTRITIONAL INFORMATION:

Calories: 272 Kcal | Protein: 21 g | Carbohydrates: 26 g | Fat: 8 g | Fiber: 2 g

Prep. Time:	Total Time:	Servings:	Difficulty Level:
10 min.	4 hrs. 10 min.	8	Medium

DIRECTIONS

Add diced onion, olive oil, and garlic to the slow cooker's bottom. Then add salt, chicken breasts, and pepper, as well as the rice. Add 2/3 of the broth container. Stir. Turn the slow cooker on high and cover it. Cook on high for four hours. Check to see whether there is enough liquid inside after two hours. If necessary, add additional warmed broth. Stir in the chopped broccoli half an hour before it's done. If necessary, add additional heated broth. Cook for another 30 minutes until the broccoli is green and soft. Stir in the cheese until it melts. If desired, season with additional salt and pepper. Serve right away.

Seafood Recipes

BLACKENED SALMON

INGREDIENTS

- 1 Tablespoon of olive oil or butter
- 4 6 oz salmon fillets; skin-on
- 3 Tablespoons of blackened seasoning /Cajun seasoning
- 2 cups of white, brown /cauliflower rice; for serving.
- Pineapple salsa; for serving.

NUTRITIONAL INFORMATION:

Calories: 485 Kcal | Protein: 46 g | Carbohydrates: 30 g | Fat: 19 g | Fiber: 3 g

Prep. Time:	Total Time:	Servings:	Difficulty Level:
10 min.	20 min.	4	Medium

DIRECTIONS

If necessary, make a blackened seasoning. Apply a generous amount of blackened seasoning to each salmon fillet's meat. Heat the oil or butter in a wide nonstick /cast iron pan over medium heat. Cook the fillets, skin-side up, in the pan until browned, for approximately 3 minutes. Cook, flipping once or twice until the fillets are cooked to your liking, for around 5 to 7 minutes, depending on the thickness of the fillets. Serve over rice with pineapple salsa on top.

GARLIC SHRIMP AND ASPARAGUS WITH ZUCCHINI NOODLES

INGREDIENTS

- 1 lb. asparagus; trimmed and chopped.
- 1 Tablespoon of olive oil
- ½ teaspoon of sea salt
- 5 minced garlic cloves
- ¼-1 teaspoon of crushed red pepper
- 1 lb. peeled and deveined shrimp.
- ¼ teaspoon of black pepper; freshly ground.
- 2 Tablespoons of fresh lemon juice
- parsley for garnish; fresh chopped
- 2 medium zucchinis; spiralized into noodles

NUTRITIONAL INFORMATION:

Calories: 321 Kcal | Protein: 37 g | Carbohydrates: 23 g | Fat: 9 g | Fiber: 8 g

Prep. Time:	Total Time:	Servings:	Difficulty Level:
10 min.	20 min.	2	Medium

DIRECTIONS

In a wide nonstick skillet, heat the oil over medium heat. Add salt, asparagus, red pepper, garlic, and black pepper, and cook for 2 minutes. Cook, often stirring, for approximately 4 minutes after adding the shrimp. Add the lemon juice and mix well. Transfer the mixture to a dish and put it aside after the shrimp is cooked.

Sauté zucchini noodles in the same skillet for 1-2 minutes before returning the shrimp and asparagus combination to the pan. Stir to incorporate everything, remove it from the heat, and serve with fresh parsley.

SUPERFOOD BAKED SALMON

INGREDIENTS

- 2 cups of brussels sprouts (quartered)
- 3 to 4 salmon fillets; (4–5 ounces each)
- 1/4 to 1/3 olive oil
- 1/4 to 1/3 cup of chopped fresh basil.
- 1 cup of fresh blueberries
- 3 tbsp of balsamic vinegar
- 1/4 to 1/2 tsp of crushed black Pepper
- 2 cloves / 1 tsp of minced Garlic
- 2 Lemons; one juiced & one sliced
- Sea Salt

NUTRITIONAL INFORMATION:

Calories: 395Kcal | Protein: 23.7 g | Carbohydrates: 12.4 g | Fat: 28.1 g | Fiber: 2.8 g

Prep. Time:	Total Time:	Servings:	Difficulty Level:
5 min.	20 min.	4	Medium

DIRECTIONS

Preheat the oven to 400 degrees Fahrenheit. Clean salmon fillets and put them on a parchment-lined baking sheet. Brussels sprouts should be cleaned and chopped. Place them in the pan. Season the salmon and vegetables with a generous amount of sea salt. Set it aside. Put blueberries in a bowl. Using a fork, mash a little. Add 1/4 teaspoon of salt, basil, 1/4 cup of extra virgin olive oil, 1/4 teaspoon of pepper, garlic, and balsamic vinegar. Combine all of the ingredients. Drizzle 2 to 3 tablespoons of extra virgin olive oil over the fish and Brussels sprouts. Over the salmon fillets, spoon the balsamic basil blueberry mixture.

Fresh lemon juice should be squeezed over the fish and vegetables. On the sheet pan, place lemon slices on top of the vegetables. Add black pepper if desired, and bake for 15 minutes. Broil for 1 to 2 minutes to crisp up the baked salmon skin and Brussels sprouts. Remove the dish from the oven. Serve and have fun!

ROASTED SALMON, SMOKY CHICKPEAS, AND GREENS

INGREDIENTS

- 1 tablespoon of smoked paprika
- 2 tablespoons of olive oil; extra-virgin, divided.
- 1 can (15 ounces) of chickpeas; salt-free, rinsed
- ½ teaspoon of salt; divided and a pinch.
- ¼ cup of fresh chopped chives/dill, and more for garnish
- ⅓ cup of buttermilk
- ¼ cup of mayonnaise
- ¼ teaspoon of garlic powder
- ½ teaspoon of ground pepper, divided.
- 10 cups of chopped kale
- 1¼ pound of wild salmon; 4 portions
- ¼ cup of water

NUTRITIONAL INFORMATION:

Calories: 447 Kcal | Protein: 37 g | Carbohydrates: 23.4 g | Fat: 21.8 g | Fiber: 6.4 g

Prep. Time:	Total Time:	Servings:	Difficulty Level:
30 min.	40 min.	4	Medium

DIRECTIONS

Preheat an oven to 425 degrees F, with racks in the top third and center. Mix paprika, 1 tablespoon of oil, and 1/4 teaspoon salt in a medium mixing dish. Toss the chickpeas with the paprika mixture after completely drying them. Spread the mixture on the rimmed baking sheet. Bake the chickpeas for 30 minutes on the top rack, stirring twice.

Meanwhile, mix the mayonnaise in a blender, 1/4 teaspoon of pepper, buttermilk, herbs, and garlic powder until smooth. Put it aside. In a large pan, heat the remaining 1 tablespoon of oil over medium heat. Cook, stirring periodically, for 2 minutes after adding the greens. Add and cook kale, occasionally stirring, until soft, for approximately 5 minutes longer. Remove the pan from the heat and add a pinch of salt.

Take the chickpeas out of the oven and place them on one side of the pan. Put salmon on another side of the pan and season the salmon with the remaining 1/4 tsp of salt and pepper. Bake for 5 to 8 minutes or until the salmon is cooked through. Serve the salmon with the greens and chickpeas, drizzling the leftover dressing on top and garnishing with additional herbs if preferred.

SHEET PAN TURMERIC SALMON WITH CHERRY SAUCE

INGREDIENTS

- 1/2 teaspoon of cinnamon
- 1-pound wild salmon
- 1/2 teaspoon of kosher salt
- 1 teaspoon of turmeric
- 1 bunch of broccolis rabe; washed & ends trimmed.
- 1/4 teaspoon of garlic powder
- 1-2 tablespoons of olive oil; extra virgin
- 1/4 teaspoon of black pepper; freshly ground.

For The Cherry Sauce:
- 2 minced cloves garlic,
- 1 1/2 cups of frozen cherries
- 1 tablespoon of water
- 1/2 tablespoon of lemon juice
- 1/2 teaspoon of arrowroot powder
- salt and pepper; to taste.

Prep. Time:	Total Time:	Servings:	Difficulty Level:
10 min.	25 min.	4	Medium

DIRECTIONS

Preheat the oven to 425 degrees Fahrenheit. In a small dish, combine the spices. Place the salmon on a large baking sheet and rub the spice mixture over it. Surround the fish with broccoli rabe. Drizzle olive oil and leftover spice combination over the broccoli. Place it in the oven for 10-15 mins, or until salmon is cooked and broccoli rabe begins to wilt to your taste.

For the cherry sauce

Add garlic, frozen cherries, pepper, salt, and lemon juice in a small saucepan over medium heat. Once the cherries are cooking, use a spatula to split them up. Cook until most of the water has evaporated. In a small dish, combine the water and arrowroot powder. Reduce heat, add to the cherry mixture, and whisk for 30 sec before removing from the heat. Serve on top of fish that has been cooked.

NUTRITIONAL INFORMATION:

Calories: 304 Kcal | Protein: 32 g | Carbohydrates: 8 g | Fat: 16 g | Fiber: 2 g

CREAMY SUNDRIED TOMATO PAN SEARED SOLE

INGREDIENTS

- 2 tbsp. of olive oil; extra virgin
- 1 tsp. of dried thyme
- 2 sole fillets
- ½ cup of vegetable broth
- 2 tbsp. of minced garlic
- salt & pepper; to taste.
- ¼ cup of sundried tomatoes

Prep. Time:	Total Time:	Servings:	Difficulty Level:
5 min.	20 min.	2	Medium

DIRECTIONS

In a large pan, warm extra virgin olive oil over medium heat. Add broth, minced garlic, and sundried tomatoes. Cook for another 2-3 minutes, and add salt, sole fillets, and pepper. Add and cook fillets for 3 minutes. Cook for another 3 minutes with the lid on the pan. Reduce the heat to low and add the dried thyme.

NUTRITIONAL INFORMATION:

Calories: 300 Kcal | Protein: 14 g | Carbohydrates: 47 g | Fat: 6 g | Fiber: 7 g

FISH CEVICHE

INGREDIENTS

- 1 cucumber
- ½ small red onion
- 1 small mango
- 2 lbs. haddock/ codfish
- 1 tbsp of sea salt
- 9 limes
- 1½ tbsp of pink peppercorn
- ½ bunch of cilantro
- 1 small slice of watermelon
- 2 serrano peppers
- 1 tbsp of EVOO

NUTRITIONAL INFORMATION:

Calories: 82 Kcal | Protein: 15 g | Carbohydrates: 2.6 g | Fat: 1.3 g | Fiber: 0.5 g

Prep. Time:	Total Time:	Servings:	Difficulty Level:
25 min.	30 min.	2	Medium

DIRECTIONS

Cut fish into approximately 1/2-inch-long pieces and blanch it for 3 minutes in boiling water, take it out, and cool it on ice. Put the fish in a bowl. Add 1 tbsp of EVOO and the juice of 5 limes. Allow 10 minutes to marinate in the refrigerator. Meanwhile, combine the pink peppercorn, sea salt, coarsely chopped serrano pepper, cilantro, and cucumber in a mortar and pestle. One lime should be squeezed, and everything should be ground until it resembles an Italian pesto (or use a food processor or blender).

Put the remaining diced cucumber (with skin on) in a dish and cubed mango. Squeeze the remaining limes and add red onion and finely chopped cilantro. Toss together all of the ingredients. Add avocado and marinated fish (and watermelon if using). Mix everything with care. For 5 minutes in the refrigerator, chill it before serving.

THAI GREEN CURRY WITH SHRIMP AND KALE

INGREDIENTS

- 1 tablespoon of chopped fresh garlic.
- 2 teaspoons of olive oil
- 1 tablespoon of chopped fresh ginger.
- ⅓ cup of chopped green onions.
- 1¼ cups of matchstick-cut carrots
- 2 tablespoons of Thai green curry paste
- 1 (13.5-ounce) can of light coconut milk
- ½ cup of unsalted chicken stock
- 6 cups of packed Lacinato kale; chopped (about 1/2 bunch)
- 1 pound of medium shrimp; peeled and deveined
- ¼ teaspoon of kosher salt
- 6 ounces of dried rice noodles
- ¼ cup of chopped fresh cilantro.
- 1½ teaspoons of fresh lime juice
- 1 teaspoon of grated lime rind

NUTRITIONAL INFORMATION:

Calories: 398 Kcal | Protein: 20 g | Carbohydrates: 60 g | Fat: 9.7 g | Fiber: 4 g

Prep. Time:	Total Time:	Servings:	Difficulty Level:
15 min.	25 min.	4	Medium

DIRECTIONS

Prepare rice noodles as directed on the box. Rinse them with cold water after draining; drain them and put them aside. In a wide skillet, heat the oil over medium-high heat. Sauté garlic, green onions, and ginger for 1 minute. Stir in the curry paste and cook for another 30 seconds. Add chicken stock, carrots, and coconut milk; bring to a boil, and cook for 5 minutes.

Add kale and season with salt. Cook for 3 minutes or until the kale is soft and wilted. Add and cook shrimp for 3 minutes or until cooked through. Remove from the heat and serve with lime rind, cilantro, and juice on top. Serve with rice noodles on the side.

Vegetable Recipes

VEGAN ROASTED PUMPKIN CURRY

INGREDIENTS

- 1 onion
- 2 Tbsp of coconut oil (grape seed oil)
- 2 Tbsp of fresh ginger minced.
- 1 pumpkin/butternut squash; peeled and cubed.
- 2 Tbsp of garlic minced.
- 1 can of coconut milk; full fat
- 2 Tbsp of a curry spice blend
- 1 tsp of salt
- 200 g firm tofu
- 2 Tbsp of lemon juice

Serve
- 2/3 cup of roasted cashews
- coconut yogurt
- flatbread
- chopped parsley.

NUTRITIONAL INFORMATION:

Calories: 110 Kcal | Protein: 1.9 g | Carbohydrates: 9.1 g | Fat: 7.5 g | Fiber: 2.5 g

Prep. Time:	Total Time:	Servings:	Difficulty Level:
15 min.	45 min.	4	Medium

DIRECTIONS

To begin, preheat the oven to 220 degrees Celsius. Scrape and cube the pumpkin, then place it on a baking pan with a little oil coating. Bake for at least 20 minutes or until tender. In the meanwhile, warm a wide saucepan over medium-high heat. Add the onion, coconut oil, and ginger once the pan is heated. Cook, stirring regularly, for 2-3 minutes. Cook for an additional 2 minutes after adding the curry spice mix.

After that, add garlic and continue to sauté for a minute. Then, over medium heat, add coconut milk and bring to a simmer. Reduce heat and cover after it has reached a simmering point. Cook, stirring periodically, for 5 minutes.

Check the pumpkin at this point; if it's soft, put it in a blender and puree it with a little water until smooth. Add this puree with coconut milk to the pan and season with lemon juice and salt to taste.

Set aside and cook cubed tofu in 3 tbsp coconut oil until it develops a lovely golden crust. Serve with rice, flatbread, quinoa, or buckwheat as a side dish. Adding cashews, coconut yogurt, and parsley to the serving dish elevates the meal. Fresh is best, but leftovers may be kept in the refrigerator for up to 3 days. Enjoy!

RATATOUILLE

INGREDIENTS

- 2 sprigs of oregano
- 2 smashed garlic cloves,
- 5 tablespoons of olive oil
- 2 medium thickly sliced summer squash,
- 1 small thickly sliced eggplant,
- 2 medium thickly sliced zucchini,
- 1 cup of tomato puree (or tomato sauce)
- 2 small halved red bell peppers; sides cut off.
- 1 medium thickly sliced red onion,
- 3 medium thickly sliced tomatoes,
- Salt and black pepper; freshly ground.
- 2 tablespoons of thyme leaves

NUTRITIONAL INFORMATION:

Calories: 283 kcal | Protein: 6 g | Carbohydrates: 30 g | Fat: 18 g | Fiber: 4 g

Prep. Time:	Total Time:	Servings:	Difficulty Level:
55 min.	1 hr. 10 min.	4	Easy

DIRECTIONS

Preheat the oven to 375 degrees Fahrenheit. Place four pans or 1 9-inch square baking dish on a baking sheet. Heat olive oil and garlic in a small saucepan over medium-low heat. Cook for 1 minute or until aromatic. Remove the saucepan from the heat, add oregano, and cook it for 15 minutes. Garlic and oregano should be removed and discarded. Add 2 teaspoons of olive oil to the bottom of each baking dish. Add 2 tablespoons of tomato puree to the bottom of each baking dish. Layer the onion, eggplant, summer squash, pepper, zucchini, and tomato in the prepared baking pan. Don't worry about flawless or matching the slices; make sure they're all packed in firmly. Drizzle the remaining oil equally over the top, then brush the remaining tomato puree. Season with salt & pepper and a sprig of thyme. Roast for 25 to 30 minutes until soft and brown on the top and edges. Allow 5 to 10 minutes to cool before serving.

CURRY TOFU

INGREDIENTS

- 1 tablespoon of olive oil
- 1 teaspoon of curry powder
- 1-pound cubed tofu,
- 1 teaspoon of grated lemon zest,
- ½ cup of coconut cream

NUTRITIONAL INFORMATION:

Calories: 180 kcal | Protein: 10.1 g | Carbohydrates: 4 g | Fat: 15.5 g | Fiber: 1.9 g

Prep. Time:	Total Time:	Servings:	Difficulty Level:
20 min.	25 min.	4	Easy

DIRECTIONS

Combine curry powder, coconut cream, olive oil, and lemon zest in a mixing bowl. Then add the tofu and thoroughly combine. Allow 10 minutes for the mixture to marinade. The skillet should be properly preheated. Cook the tofu for 2 minutes on each side.

CARROT GINGER SOUP

INGREDIENTS

• 2 pounds peeled and chopped carrots,
• 1 medium diced yellow onion,
• 3 minced cloves of garlic,
• 1 tablespoon of grated fresh ginger,
• 1/2 teaspoon of turmeric
• 1 (15-oz) can of full-fat coconut milk; divided
• 1 teaspoon of ground cumin
• 1 1/2 teaspoons of salt; to taste.
• Pinch of cayenne pepper; optional
• 32 ounces of vegetable broth; low sodium

NUTRITIONAL INFORMATION:

Calories: 210 kcal | Protein: 5 g | Carbohydrates: 29 g | Fat: 9 g | Fiber: 7 g

Prep. Time:	Total Time:	Servings:	Difficulty Level:
10 min.	40 min.	6	Easy

DIRECTIONS

Add 1/2 cup of coconut milk, carrots, onion, grated ginger, cumin, garlic, and turmeric, in a large saucepan, and sauté over medium heat until carrots soften and everything is aromatic approximately 8 minutes. You can speed up the process by covering the pot and stirring occasionally.

Add vegetable broth and remaining coconut milk. Raise the heat to high and bring the mixture to a full boil. Reduce to low heat and cover, and cook for about 20 to 30 minutes or until carrots are tender.

Transfer everything to a blender and mix until smooth (this may need to be done in stages). Let the steam escape by gently opening the steam vent at the top of the lid, then mix at medium speed.

Unless the soup is already at the appropriate temperature, return the smooth carrot soup to the saucepan and cook for a few minutes. If you must reheat the soup on the stove, do it carefully; else, your tasty soup will turn into a cauldron of boiling, spurting lava.

Serve with a dollop of coconut milk yogurt, fresh cilantro, sesame seeds, and a drizzle of coconut milk.

CUMIN ZUCCHINI RINGS

INGREDIENTS

- 1 tablespoon of cumin seeds
- 3 sliced zucchinis,
- ¼ teaspoon of cayenne pepper
- 1 tablespoon of olive oil

NUTRITIONAL INFORMATION:

Calories: 48 kcal | Protein: 1.6 g | Carbohydrates: 4.5 g | Fat: 3.3 g | Fiber: 1.4 g

Prep. Time:	Total Time:	Servings:	Difficulty Level:
25 min.	15 min.	4	Easy

DIRECTIONS

The baking paper should be used to line the baking pan. Arrange zucchini slices in a single layer on the baking pan. Olive oil, cumin seeds, and cayenne pepper are then sprinkled on top and baked at 360°F for 15 minutes.

BROCCOLI SOUP

INGREDIENTS

- 1/4 cup of diced celery
- 1 1/2 cups of chopped broccoli
- 1/4 cup of chopped onion
- 2 cups of nonfat milk
- 1 cup of chicken broth; low-sodium
- 2 tablespoons of cornstarch
- 1 dash of pepper
- 1/4 teaspoon of salt
- 1/4 cup of grated Swiss cheese
- 1 dash of ground thyme

NUTRITIONAL INFORMATION:

Calories: 118 kcal | Protein: 9.5 g | Carbohydrates: 15.9 g | Fat: 2.6 g | Fiber: 2 g

Prep. Time:	Total Time:	Servings:	Difficulty Level:
10 min.	30 min.	4	Easy

DIRECTIONS

In a saucepan, add the veggies and broth. Bring to a boil, then reduce to low heat and simmer until the veggies are soft, approximately 8 minutes. Combine the pepper, milk, salt, cornstarch, and thyme in a mixing bowl; stir in the cooked veggies.

Cook, stirring continuously, for approximately 5 minutes or until the soup has gently thickened and the mixture has just started to boil. Remove the pan from the heat. Stir in the cheese until it is completely melted.

INSTANT POT POTATO LEEK SOUP

INGREDIENTS

- 1 small diced onion,
- 2 tablespoons of grapeseed oil
- 3-4 minced cloves of garlic,
- 3 medium cleaned & sliced leeks ; (white and light green parts)
- ½ teaspoon of dried rosemary
- ¾ teaspoon of dried thyme
- 5 small peeled and chopped russet potatoes (2 pounds)
- ½ teaspoon of ground coriander
- 4 cups of vegetable broth; low sodium
- 1 teaspoon of salt; more to taste
- 2 bay leaves
- 1 cup of canned coconut milk
- Fresh ground pepper; to taste.

NUTRITIONAL INFORMATION:

Calories: 364 kcal | Protein: 9 g | Carbohydrates: 44 g | Fat: 13 g | Fiber: 4 g

Prep. Time:	Total Time:	Servings:	Difficulty Level:
20 min.	26 min.	5	Easy

DIRECTIONS

Add the oil to Instant Pot and turn ON the sauté command. Add the onions and leeks once the oil is hot. Sauté for 4-6 minutes or until softened. Add rosemary, garlic, thyme, and coriander. Sauté for 30-60 seconds or until aromatic.

Turn OFF the sauté function. Add vegetable broth, potatoes, salt, bay leaf, and pepper. Close the lid and fasten it. The steam release handle should be in the Sealing position. Adjust the Pressure Cooker to high pressure and use the + or - buttons to set the duration to 6 minutes.

When the time is up, the cooker will beep. Turn the steam release handle to the Venting position with care (It will spurt out steam and water). You may open the lid after the Float Valve has gone down.

After removing the bay leaves, pour coconut milk. Process it until smooth and creamy with an immersion blender (or a normal blender). Season to taste. If the soup is too thick, thin it down with a little quantity of vegetable broth.

SORREL SOUP

INGREDIENTS

- 1 cup of chopped spinach,
- 2 cups of chopped sorrel,
- 1 chopped onion,
- 2 cups of chopped cauliflower,
- 8 cups of water
- 1 teaspoon of dried basil
- 4 cups of chopped tomatoes,
- 1 tablespoon of avocado oil

NUTRITIONAL INFORMATION:

Calories: 38 kcal | Protein: 2.2 g | Carbohydrates: 7.4 g | Fat: 0.7 g | Fiber: 3.1 g

Prep. Time:	Total Time:	Servings:	Difficulty Level:
10 min.	40 min.	8	Easy

DIRECTIONS

In a pan, pour oil. On medium heat, add onion and roast it for 3-4 minutes. Then add the tomatoes, cauliflower, and dry basil. Add water and cook the soup for 10 minutes after. After that, add the sorrel and boil the soup for another 16 minutes. Allow time for the soup to cool before serving.

Chapter 6:
Main Courses
Meat Recipes

CHICKEN TERIYAKI RICE

INGREDIENTS

- 2 teaspoons of olive oil; extra virgin
- 1 cup of white rice
- 1 1/2 Tablespoons of olive oil; extra virgin
- 1 1/2 pounds of organic boneless, skinless chicken breasts
- 1 red bell pepper; sliced thin.
- 1 large, sweet onion; sliced thin.

For the sauce
- 1/2 cup of honey
- 1 teaspoon of ginger
- 1/2 cup of pineapple juice
- 1 Tablespoon of brown sugar
- 1/2 cup of gluten-free tamari
- pinch of red pepper flakes
- 4 green onions; sliced white and green parts,

NUTRITIONAL INFORMATION:

Calories: 432 Kcal | Protein: 29 g | Carbohydrates: 57 g | Fat: 9 g | Fiber: 1 g

Prep. Time:	Total Time:	Servings:	Difficulty Level:
10 min.	45 min.	6	Medium

DIRECTIONS

Fill a big saucepan halfway with water and add the chicken breasts. Bring it to a boil with the cover on the pan. Reduce heat to low and cook for 20-30 minutes until the chicken is cooked completely and the internal temperature reaches 170 degrees F. Take the chicken out of the pan and put it aside to cool. Once the chicken has cooled, shred it with your hands or two forks.

Make the rice while the chicken is cooking: In a saucepan, combine 1 cup of white long-grain rice, 1 1/2 cups of water, and 2 tablespoons of olive oil. Bring it to a boil, lower it to low heat, and cover. Cook for approximately 25 minutes or until the rice is soft and fluffy.

Meanwhile, combine the sliced red pepper, chopped onion, and 1 1/2 tablespoons of olive oil in a pan. Cook, occasionally stirring, until the vegetables are soft and gently caramelized, approximately 30 minutes.

Make the sauce once the chicken, rice, and vegetables are done. In a small saucepan, combine the honey, tamari, ginger, pineapple juice, and brown sugar. Bring to a low simmer over medium heat. Allow 5 minutes of cooking time. Add the red pepper flakes and mix well.

Combine the shredded chicken, onions, rice, and peppers in a large mixing bowl. Pour the sauce over the top and mix everything. Serve immediately with a sprinkling of chopped green onions on top. If you have access to sesame seeds, sprinkle a few on top of each dish.

SLOW COOKER DAIRY-FREE BUTTER CHICKEN

INGREDIENTS

- 1-inch chopped knob of ginger.
- 2 Tablespoons of Coconut Oil
- 1 tablespoon of garam masala
- 5 minced cloves of garlic
- 1 Tablespoon of cumin
- 2 teaspoons of ground turmeric
- 1 teaspoon of chili powder
- 1/2 teaspoon of ground pepper
- 1 teaspoon of sea salt
- 1/2 teaspoon of cayenne, optional
- 2 lb. skinless, boneless chicken breast; chunks
- 1/2 teaspoon of ground cinnamon
- 15 oz can of coconut milk; full fat
- 1 cinnamon stick
- 15 oz can of tomato sauce
- 1 chopped yellow onion.
- 2 Tablespoons of lemon juice
- 1/4 cup of chopped cilantro
- 2 cups of frozen green beans; thawed, optional.

NUTRITIONAL INFORMATION:

Calories: 304 Kcal | Protein: 28 g | Carbohydrates: 9 g | Fat: 18 g | Fiber: 2 g

Prep. Time:	Total Time:	Servings:	Difficulty Level:
10 min.	6 hrs.	8	Medium

DIRECTIONS

Cook onion and garlic in oil in a wide skillet or saucepan until soft and aromatic for approximately 5 minutes. Add turmeric, fresh ginger, garam masala, chili powder, cumin, salt, cinnamon, pepper, and cayenne. Cook for 1-2 minutes more.

Add onion and garlic combination in a slow cooker. Then add tomato sauce, chicken, lemon juice, coconut milk, and cinnamon stick.

Cook on a high for 3 hours or on low for 6 hours, covered. Add the green beans when there's approximately an hour remaining in the cooking process.

Serve butter chicken with fresh cilantro and a lemon slice for squeezing over the cauliflower rice (normal rice).

BOILED CHICKEN

INGREDIENTS

- 3 unpeeled carrots, smash into chunks
- 1 whole chicken (3 pounds)
- 2 stalks of celery, smash into chunks
- 1 large unpeeled halved onion,
- water to cover.
- 1 tablespoon of whole peppercorns

NUTRITIONAL INFORMATION:

Calories: 186 Kcal | Protein: 16.3 g | Carbohydrates: 4.5 g | Fat: 11.1 g | Fiber:3 g

Prep. Time:	Total Time:	Servings:	Difficulty Level:
1 hr.	1 hr. 40 min.	8	Medium

DIRECTIONS

In a large saucepan, combine the onion, chicken, celery, carrots, and peppercorns, and cover with water. Then, boil, lower to low heat, and simmer for 90 minutes until the chicken flesh falls from the bone. Remove the chicken and set it aside to cool before shredding or chopping the flesh.

GRILLED CURRY CHICKEN

INGREDIENTS

• 1 1/2 lbs. skinless, boneless chicken breasts

Thai Curry Spice Blend
• 1/2 Tablespoon of onion powder
• 2 1/2 Tablespoons of curry powder
• 2-3 teaspoons of red pepper flakes; crushed.
• 1 teaspoon of dried parsley
• 1 1/2 teaspoons of sea salt

NUTRITIONAL INFORMATION:

Calories: 212 Kcal | Protein: 37 g | Carbohydrates: 3 g | Fat: 5 g | Fiber:3 g

Prep. Time:	Total Time:	Servings:	Difficulty Level:
15 min.	25 min.	4	Medium

DIRECTIONS

To make the spice mix, combine the onion powder, curry powder, sea salt, crushed red pepper flakes, and parsley in a small bowl. Use as much spice mix as you need to coat each chicken breast. You may have some spice rub left over; store it in an airtight jar for later use. Just make sure you don't get any raw chicken juice on it.

Preheat a medium-hot indoor or outdoor grill. Lightly spray the grill grate, put the chicken on it, and cook for 5 to 6 minutes on each side or until the juices flow clearly. The time it takes to cook a chicken breast depends on its size.

BEEFY BAKE CASSEROLE

INGREDIENTS

• 1/8 tsp of pepper
• 1 1/2 cups of gluten-free elbow macaroni, if needed
• 1 8 oz tomato sauce
• 1 lb. lean ground turkey, ground beef, or chicken
• 1 6 oz tomato paste
• 1/2-3/4 cup of celery finely; chopped.
• 1 cup of water
• 1/2 cup of onion; finely chopped.
• 1/4 tsp of chili powder
• 1/2 tsp of salt
• 1 cup of grated cheddar cheese/ more if desired
• 1 1/2 cups of frozen corn

NUTRITIONAL INFORMATION:

Calories: 473 Kcal | Protein: 35 g | Carbohydrates: 55 g | Fat: 13 g | Fiber:6 g

Prep. Time:	Total Time:	Servings:	Difficulty Level:
20 min.	50 min.	4	Medium

DIRECTIONS

Cook macaroni as per package instructions. Drain it and put it aside for 10-11 minutes. Brown the meat in the pan, eliminate fat, and add the onions and celery. Cook for approximately 5 minutes together. Except for the noodles, add all ingredients. Mix thoroughly. Add the noodles and toss them together gently. Sprinkle 1 cup of shredded cheddar cheese after pouring the macaroni into a 2 1/2-quart casserole and bake for 30 minutes at 350 degrees F

KUNG PAO CHICKEN

INGREDIENTS

- 4 minced cloves of garlic
- 1 lb. skinless, boneless chopped chicken breast; chunks
- 2 teaspoons of fresh ginger minced or grated.
- 1 Tablespoon of sesame oil divided.
- 3 cups of broccoli
- 1 chopped bell pepper orange, yellow, or red,
- 2 chopped green onions.
- crushed peanuts; for serving (optional)
- 2 cups of cooked brown rice; for serving.

Sauce
- 1-2 Tablespoons of honey
- 1/4 cup of coconut aminos / soy sauce; low sodium /tamari
- 1/2-1 teaspoon of arrowroot powder; for thickening, optional
- 2 teaspoons of chili sambal Oelek paste/ sriracha.

NUTRITIONAL INFORMATION:

Calories: 340 Kcal | Protein: 27 g | Carbohydrates: 43 g | Fat: 8 g | Fiber:5 g

Prep. Time:	Total Time:	Servings:	Difficulty Level:
10 min.	25 min.	4	Medium

DIRECTIONS

To make the sauce, whisk together the ingredients in a small bowl.

In a large sauté pan or wok, heat 1/2 tbsp of sesame oil. When the pan is heated, add garlic, chicken, and ginger, and cook for 5-7 minutes or until the chicken is finished. Place the chicken on a platter. Toss the remaining oil, green onions, bell pepper, and broccoli in the same pan. Simmer for 5 minutes, or until broccoli is soft; add sauce and the chicken to the pan and cook for another 2-3 minutes, or until sauce thickens. Remove from heat and set aside for 2-3 minutes.

Over brown rice, serve vegetables and kung pao chicken. For spicier, top with sriracha and crushed peanuts.

CHICKEN PICCATA WITH GARLICKY GREENS & NEW POTATOES

INGREDIENTS

- 300g green beans; trimmed
- 200g new potatoes; halved or quartered
- 2 skinless chicken breasts
- 200g spring greens; shredded
- 1 tbsp of drained capers
- 3 tsp of olive oil
- 1 lemon; zested and juiced
- 100ml chicken stock /water
- 1 tbsp of grated parmesan
- 2 small garlic cloves; sliced

NUTRITIONAL INFORMATION:

Calories: 393 kcal | Protein: 41 g | Carbohydrates: 22 g | Fat: 13 g | Fiber: 13 g

Prep. Time:	Total Time:	Servings:	Difficulty Level:
5 min.	20 min.	2	Easy

DIRECTIONS

In a large saucepan of boiling salted water, cook the fresh potatoes for 8-10 minutes or until cooked. For the final 3 minutes, add the spring greens and green beans. Drain and separate the greens from the potatoes.

While the potatoes are boiling, cut the chicken breasts lengthwise through the middle, leaving one side intact, so the breasts spread out like a book. Season with salt and pepper after brushing each with 1 tsp olive oil.

Cook chicken for 4 minutes on each side in a large frying pan over medium-high heat until browned. Pour in the capers, stock, lemon juice, and zest, and reduce the sauce slowly for a few minutes. Cook for another minute after adding the cooked potatoes.

In a separate frying pan, heat the remaining 1 tsp oil and cook the garlic for 1 minute or until gently brown and aromatic. Add the drained greens in garlicky oil and mix to combine. Season with salt and pepper, then top with parmesan cheese and serve with the chicken and potatoes.

APPLE CIDER VINEGAR CHICKEN

INGREDIENTS

• 2 Tablespoons of Italian seasoning
• 1/4 pound of skinless, boneless chicken breasts
• 1 Tablespoon of olive oil
• 1/4 cup of apple cider vinegar
• 1/2 teaspoon of ground pepper
• 1 teaspoon of sea salt

NUTRITIONAL INFORMATION:

Calories: 223 Kcal | Protein: 39 g | Carbohydrates: 1 g | Fat: 6 g | Fiber:3 g

Prep. Time:	Total Time:	Servings:	Difficulty Level:
1 hr.	1 hr. 15 min.	3	Medium

DIRECTIONS

Mix the Italian seasoning, vinegar, salt, oil, and pepper in a mixing bowl. Place the chicken in a shallow dish or a 1-gallon plastic bag that can be sealed.

Refrigerate for about 1 hour or 12 hours after adding the marinade and tossing to coat. Remove the chicken from the marinade, shake off any excess, and discard the rest. Preheat a grill pan or a grill. Place the chicken on the grill once it's hot and cook for 5 minutes on each side or until it's cooked completely and no longer pink.

You may alternatively broil the chicken if you don't have a barbecue. Spray a broiler pan with cooking spray before lining it with foil. Put the chicken on a foil-lined baking sheet. Broil, keep an eye on it, so it doesn't burn. After approximately 5 minutes, flip the chicken. Cook for 10-15 minutes or until chicken is no longer pink and cooked through.

Enjoy the chicken right now, or chill it down, put it in storage containers, and preserve it for later.

Seafood Recipes

MANGO SHRIMP KEBABS

INGREDIENTS

- ½ teaspoon of salt
- 2 limes; cut into wedges.
- 1½ pound large shrimp; peeled and deveined
- 2 large red bell peppers; 1-inch pieces
- ⅛ teaspoon of black pepper; freshly ground.
- 2 peeled mangoes; 1-inch cubes
- Cooking spray
- 1 small red onion; 1-inch pieces

Prep. Time:	Total Time:	Servings:	Difficulty Level:
10 min.	20 min.	4	Medium

DIRECTIONS

Heat the grill to medium-high heat. Season the shrimp with pepper and salt to taste. Using 8 (12-inch) skewers, alternately thread mango, bell pepper, shrimp, and onion pieces. Grill for 2 minutes on each side, or until shrimp are done, on a grill rack sprayed with cooking spray. Lime wedges should be squeezed over the kebabs.

NUTRITIONAL INFORMATION:

Calories: 277 Kcal | Protein: 35.8 g | Carbohydrates: 27.1 g | Fat: 3.3 g | Fiber:4.2g

SALMON CHOWDER

INGREDIENTS

- ⅓ cup of chopped carrot
- 1 tablespoon of canola oil
- ⅓ cup of chopped celery
- 1½ cups of water
- 4 cups of reduced-sodium chicken broth
- 2 1/2 cups of frozen, coarsely chopped cauliflower florets, thawed.
- 1 12-ounce of skinned salmon fillet,
- Freshly ground pepper to taste.
- 1 1/3 cups of instant mashed potato flakes / 2 cups of leftover mashed potatoes
- 3 tablespoons of fresh chopped chives or scallions, / 1 1/2 tablespoons of dried chives
- 1/4 cup of chopped fresh dill, /2 teaspoons of dried tarragon.
- ¼ teaspoon of salt
- 1 tablespoon of Dijon mustard

Prep. Time:	Total Time:	Servings:	Difficulty Level:
10 min.	30 min.	6	Medium

DIRECTIONS

Heat the oil over medium heat in a medium saucepan or Dutch oven. Add and Cook, often turning, until the carrots and celery begin to brown, for about 3 to 4 minutes. Bring the cauliflower, broth, salmon, water, and chives (or onions) to a gentle boil. Cook, covered, at a low simmer for 5 to 8 minutes or until the salmon is just cooked through. Transfer the salmon to a cutting board that has been cleaned. With a fork, flake into bite-size pieces. In a large mixing bowl, combine the dill (or tarragon), potato flakes (or leftover mashed potatoes), and mustard. Reduce the heat to a low simmer. Reheat the salmon after adding it. Salt & pepper to taste.

NUTRITIONAL INFORMATION:

Calories: 178 Kcal | Protein: 17.1 g | Carbohydrates: 16.9 g | Fat: 5.6 g | Fiber:4.2g

GARLIC SALMON

INGREDIENTS

- pepper and salt to taste
- 1½ pounds of salmon fillet
- One sprig of fresh dill; chopped.
- 3 cloves of garlic; minced.
- 5 slices of lemon
- 2 chopped green onions,
- 5 sprigs of fresh dill weed.

NUTRITIONAL INFORMATION:

Calories: 169 Kcal | Protein: 24.5 g | Carbohydrates: 2.1 g | Fat: 6.7 g | Fiber: 5g

Prep. Time:	Total Time:	Servings:	Difficulty Level:
10 min.	40 min.	6	Medium

DIRECTIONS

Preheat the oven to 450 degrees Fahrenheit (230 degrees C). Using cooking spray, coat two wide sheets of aluminum foil.

Place the salmon fillet on one sheet of foil. Season the salmon with pepper, garlic, salt, and dill sprigs. Place the sprig of dill on each lemon slice after arranging the slices on top of the fillet. Chopped scallions are sprinkled over the fillet.

Cover the salmon with the second foil sheet and seal the edges together to seal it firmly. Place it in a wide baking dish or on a baking sheet. Cook for 20 to 25 mins in a preheated oven or until fish flakes easily.

CILANTRO LIME CATFISH

INGREDIENTS

- ¼ cup of fresh cilantro, chopped.
- ½ lime, juiced.
- 1 tablespoon of olive oil
- ½ teaspoon of chopped garlic
- ½ lemon, juiced.
- salt and black pepper; ground, to taste
- 5 fillets of catfish (5 ounces)

NUTRITIONAL INFORMATION:

Calories: 272 kcal | Protein: 21.8 g | Carbohydrates: 1.7 g | Fat: 19.7 g | Fiber: 4 g

Prep. Time:	Total Time:	Servings:	Difficulty Level:
5 min.	30 min.	5	Medium

DIRECTIONS

In a pan over medium heat, melt the butter. Cook garlic and cilantro for 1 minute in heated butter. Season fillets with pepper and salt, then carefully place them in the butter mixture. Cover the skillet with a lid. Cook fillets for 10 minutes, then flip and cook for another 10 minutes, or until the fish easily flakes with a fork and is gently browned. To serve, squeeze lemon and lime juice over fillets.

ROASTED ORANGE-FENNEL STRIPED BASS

INGREDIENTS

- 2 tablespoons of olive oil; extra-virgin, divided.
- 1 large fennel bulb (with stalks)
- ¾ teaspoon of kosher salt, divided.
- 6 minced garlic cloves,
- 3 tablespoons of fresh lemon juice
- 2 (1 3/4-pound) cleaned whole striped bass
- ¼ teaspoon of black pepper; freshly ground.
- 1 orange; 8 slices
- Cooking spray

NUTRITIONAL INFORMATION:

Calories: 271 Kcal | Protein: 33 g | Carbohydrates: 11 g | Fat: 10.5 g | Fiber:3 g

Prep. Time:	Total Time:	Servings:	Difficulty Level:
20 min.	45 min.	4	Medium

DIRECTIONS

Preheat the oven to 400 degrees Fahrenheit. Remove the fronds from the fennel bulb and coarsely chop them to make 1 tablespoon of fronds. Stalks should be removed and discarded. Fennel bulbs are thinly sliced. Over medium-high heat, heat the large nonstick skillet. Swirl in 1 tablespoon of oil to coat it. Add the garlic and sliced fennel to the pan and cook, often turning, for 6 minutes or until gently browned. Add 1/4 teaspoon of salt. Remove the pan from heat and set it aside to cool for 5 minutes.

Make three diagonal incisions in the skin of each fish. Whisk together the remaining 1 tablespoon of oil and the lemon juice. Half of the lemon juice mixture should be rubbed into each fish's flesh, and the other half should be drizzled outside each fish. Sprinkle the remaining 1/2 teaspoon of salt and pepper evenly within the flesh. Place each fish on a jelly-roll pan lined with parchment paper and cooking spray. Fill each fish with half of the fennel mixture and four orange slices.

Rest for 5 minutes after roasting at 400° for 30 mins /until fish flakes readily when checked with a fork. Fennel fronds, if used, should be sprinkled over the fish.

CUMIN-CRUSTED SABLEFISH

INGREDIENTS

- ½ teaspoon of salt
- 1 tablespoon of cumin seeds
- 4 (6-ounce) sablefish / white sea bass fillets
- ¼ teaspoon of black pepper; freshly ground.
- ½ teaspoon of olive oil
- 4 lemon wedges
- 2 tablespoons of fresh flat-leaf parsley; chopped.

NUTRITIONAL INFORMATION:

Calories: 331 Kcal | Protein: 22.3 g | Carbohydrates: 0.9 g | Fat: 26 g | Fiber:0.3 g

Prep. Time:	Total Time:	Servings:	Difficulty Level:
5 min.	20 min.	4	Medium

DIRECTIONS

Preheat the oven to 375 degrees Fahrenheit. In a large pan over medium heat, roast cumin seeds for 2 minutes. In a coffee or spice grinder, grind salt, cumin, and pepper until finely ground. Apply the cumin mixture over both sides of the fillets.

In a large skillet, heat the oil over medium-high heat. Add fish and cook for 2 mins on each side or until fillets are browned. Wrap foil around the pan's handle and bake the fish for 4 minutes at 375°F until easily flaked when checked with the fork. Serve fish with parsley and lemon wedges on the side.

CREAMY LEEK AND SALMON SOUP

INGREDIENTS

- 4 leeks; washed, trimmed, & sliced into crescents
- 2 tbsp of avocado oil
- 3 cloves garlic; minced
- 2 tsp of dried thyme leaves
- 6 cups of seafood /chicken broth
- 1 lb. salmon, in bitesize pieces
- Salt & pepper; to taste
- 1 3/4 cups of coconut milk

NUTRITIONAL INFORMATION:

Calories: 326 kcal | Protein: 18.7 g | Carbohydrates: 31.1 g | Fat: 25.8 g | Fiber: 3.8 g

Prep. Time:	Total Time:	Servings:	Difficulty Level:
5 min.	30 min.	4	Medium

DIRECTIONS

Heat avocado oil in a large pan or Dutch oven over low-medium heat. Add leeks and garlic and cook until slightly softened.

Add thyme and stock. Simmer for about 15 minutes, then season to taste with salt and pepper. Toss the salmon with the coconut milk in a pan. Return to low heat and simmer for approximately 10 minutes or until salmon is opaque and done. Serve immediately!

ZOODLES & GRILLED SHRIMP WITH THE LEMON BASIL DRESSING

INGREDIENTS

- 1/8 tsp of Black Pepper
- 2 1/2 cups of Zucchini
- 1/8 tsp of Salt
- 1 lb. Raw Shrimp
- 1/2 cup of Cherry Tomatoes; halved
- 1/4 cup of Almonds; sliced
- 3/4 cup of Basil
- 1 medium Shallot; chopped
- 1 small Garlic Cloves
- 1/4 tsp of Crushed Red Pepper Flakes
- 1 tbsp of Lemon Zest
- 2 tsp of Olive Oil

NUTRITIONAL INFORMATION:

Calories: 356.1 kcal | Protein: 18.4 g |
Carbohydrates: 8.1 g | Fat: 28.6 g | Fiber: 2.4 g

Prep. Time:	Total Time:	Servings:	Difficulty Level:
10 min.	22 min.	2	Medium

DIRECTIONS

In a blender, mix 1/8 cup of sliced almonds, red wine vinegar, 1 shallot, 1 garlic clove, red pepper flakes, 1/2 cup of olive oil, and lemon zest to make the lemon basil dressing. Pulse on medium until smooth and evenly mixed. Season to taste with salt & pepper and put aside.

To toast the remaining 1/8 cup of almonds, place them in a small pan over medium-high heat. Shake the pan after every few seconds until the almonds are lightly browned. Take the almonds off the fire and put them aside. Heat one tablespoon of olive oil and heat over medium-high heat. Season the shrimp with salt & pepper. Cook shrimp for 6 to 8 minutes, or until completely cooked and pink, then mix with 2 large spoonsful of lemon basil dressing. Set aside the seasoned shrimp in a separate clean dish.

Cut the zucchini into thin spaghetti-like strands using a vegetable or spiralizer mandolin. Add the zucchini noodles to the same pan as the shrimp and cook for 2 minutes over medium heat or cook. Turn off the heat. Toss the zucchini noodles with two large spoonsful of lemon basil dressing after seasoning with salt and pepper. Any leftover lemon basil dressing may be used in another dish.

Toss the zucchini noodles, seasoned shrimp, and cherry tomatoes together. Toss in toasted sliced almonds and serve.

Vegetable Recipes

CURRIED CHICKPEA LETTUCE WRAPS

INGREDIENTS

- 1 chopped spring onion,
- 1 can (about 400g) chickpeas; drained and rinsed.
- 6 mint leaves
- 1 tsp of turmeric
- 1 tsp of cumin
- 1 chopped garlic clove,
- 1 tbsp of olive oil
- 1 tbsp of sesame seeds
- 1 tsp of ground chili peppers
- 1 tbsp of flax seeds

Salad
- 12 basil leaves
- 1 avocado
- 2 chopped tomatoes,
- 1 tsp of lime juice
- 1 chopped spring onion,
- 6 Lettuce leaves; washed.
- 1 chopped garlic clove,
- 2 tbsp of crushed walnuts
- 1 chopped green pepper,

Prep. Time:	Total Time:	Servings:	Difficulty Level:
5 min.	10 min.	2	Medium

DIRECTIONS

Put chickpeas in a pan with a little water (approximately 1/4 cup), turmeric, and chili powder, and swirl to coat over medium-high heat (about 2-3 min)

Ensure no water is left in the pan before adding the other ingredients (garlic, olive oil, sesame seeds, onion, flax seeds, cumin, and mint leaves). Stir for approximately 1 minute, remove from heat, and cover with a lid.

Smash avocado and 1/2 diced tomato in a small bowl, add minced garlic, lime juice, and mix until smooth. To make it smoother, you may use a hand blender. Mix in the remainder of the salad components and additional salt to taste. For added nutrition and crunch, sprinkle crumbled walnuts over the top.

Arrange two tbsp. of chickpea filling and two tbsp. of salad in the center of a lettuce leaf. Rep approximately 5 times more and serve it.

NUTRITIONAL INFORMATION:

Calories: 416 kcal | Protein: 14 g | Carbohydrates: 45 g | Fat: 23 g | Fiber: 18 g

MEDITERRANEAN GRILLED EGGPLANT SALAD

INGREDIENTS

- 1 red bell pepper; medium
- ¼ cup of pine nuts
- ¼ cup of scallions; green part only
- 1 ¾ pound of unpeeled eggplant
- 3 tablespoons of olive oil
- 1 medium diced tomato,
- ¾ teaspoon of salt
- 2 tablespoons of fresh lemon juice
- ¼ teaspoon of black pepper; freshly ground.
- ½ cup of chopped fresh parsley.
- 1/8 teaspoon of smoked paprika
- 2 tablespoons of chopped mint leaves
- ½ teaspoon of red pepper flakes; crushed.

NUTRITIONAL INFORMATION:

Calories: 146 kcal | Protein: 3 g | Carbohydrates: 12 g | Fat: 11 g | Fiber: 5 g

Prep. Time:	Total Time:	Servings:	Difficulty Level:
30 min.	30 min.	6	Easy

DIRECTIONS

Toast pine nuts in a small heavy pan or skillet over medium heat for approximately 5 minutes, turning continuously until they become glossy and become golden brown in places. Because nuts burn quickly, keep a careful eye on them.

Red peppers should be halved and seeded. Cut the eggplant into 1-inch slabs lengthwise. Grill the veggies for approximately 15 minutes over medium heat on a charcoal or propane grill. When the grilled veggies are cool enough to handle, roughly chop them and place them in a medium serving dish. Add scallion greens, tomato, mint, lemon juice, olive oil, parsley, salt, red pepper flakes, black pepper, and smoked paprika to the same dish. Serve warm or cold, tossing gently to mix ingredients.

SWEET POTATOES WITH SWISS CHARD

INGREDIENTS

- 2 diced cloves of garlic
- 1 chopped red onion.
- 1 bunch of Swiss chard; chopped, tough stems removed.
- 2 medium sweet potatoes; wedges or rounds

Dressing:
- 1 tsp of maple syrup
- 2 Tbsp of red wine vinegar
- 1 Tbsp of grainy Dijon mustard
- sea salt and pepper; to taste.
- 1/2 cup of toasted pecans

NUTRITIONAL INFORMATION:

Calories: 169 Kcal | Protein: 3.3 g | Carbohydrates: 19.7 g | Fat: 9.1 g | Fiber: 4.2 g

Prep. Time:	Total Time:	Servings:	Difficulty Level:
10 min.	30 min.	4	Medium

DIRECTIONS

Cook the onion for a few minutes over medium heat with 1/4 cup of water before adding the garlic. Add potatoes and continue to sauté until nearly tender. Add the Swiss chard and a bit more water, then cover with the lid. Steam until soft. Meanwhile, make the dressing by whisking together the ingredients in a bowl. Transfer the Swiss chard and potatoes to a mixing bowl with the dressing and toss to incorporate. If preferred, top with pecans and serve warm or cold.

RED BEET BORSCHT

INGREDIENTS

• 1 small chopped yellow onion,
• 2 small peeled and shredded beets,
• 1 large green bell pepper and a small chopped
• 2 tablespoons of olive oil
• 1 small, shredded head of green cabbage,
• 1 8-ounce can of tomato sauce
• 4 medium peeled and shredded carrots,
• 1/2 teaspoon of salt
• 3 medium peeled and halved potatoes,
• 1/4 teaspoon of pepper
• 6 tablespoons of sour cream; for serving.
• 4 bay leaves
• 2 cups of parsley, chopped.
• 3 crushed garlic cloves,

NUTRITIONAL INFORMATION:

Calories: 224 kcal | Protein: 6 g | Carbohydrates: 40 g | Fat: 6 g | Fiber: 10 g

Prep. Time:	Total Time:	Servings:	Difficulty Level:
15 min.	1 hr. 15 min.	6	Medium

DIRECTIONS

In a skillet, heat the olive oil over medium heat. Add bell pepper and onion. Sauté until the onion begins to become transparent.

Continue to Sautee after adding shredded carrots and beets for another 4 to 5 minutes. Stir in the tomato sauce until it is well combined. Heat for an additional 2 minutes before turning off the heat.

Add salt, shredded cabbage, and pepper in a separate big saucepan. Bring to a boil with cold water, then cover and let simmer for approximately 20 minutes. Toss the halved potatoes into the cabbage pot. Cook after covering it until the potato is approximately halfway done.

Transfer the sauteed mixture to the cabbage-filled cooker. Add bay leaves, parsley, and smashed garlic. Turn off the heat after another 2 to 3 minutes of boiling.

SAUTÉED GREENS WITH FENNEL

INGREDIENTS

- 1 small head of roughly chopped fennel (about 1 cup)
- Pinch of salt and pepper
- 2 tablespoons of soft coconut oil
- 1 large head of Swiss chard, green or rainbow, chopped (6 cups)
- Pinch of ground cinnamon
- 2 tablespoons of balsamic vinegar
- ¼ teaspoon of dried thyme
- 2 tablespoons of golden raisins

NUTRITIONAL INFORMATION:

Calories: 41.5 Kcal | Protein: 1.6 g | Carbohydrates: 9.9 g | Fat: 0.2 g | Fiber: 3.6 g

Prep. Time:	Total Time:	Servings:	Difficulty Level:
15 min.	20 min.	6	Medium

DIRECTIONS

In a medium-sized pan, melt the coconut oil. Add fennel to the pan and simmer, stirring regularly, for 8-10 minutes or until softened. In the same pan, add the greens. Toss and cook for 4 minutes or until wilted.

Add balsamic vinegar, thyme, golden raisins, and cinnamon. Toss the coat evenly. Cook for a minute or two or until the vinegar bubbles and caramelize. Season to taste with salt and pepper. Serve at room temperature or warm.

STUFFED PEPPERS

INGREDIENTS

- 1 medium chopped onion
- 3 large red peppers; half lengthwise, seeds removed.
- 8 oz sliced mushroom
- 2 chopped cloves of garlic.
- 1 1/2 cups of cooked brown rice/ quinoa,
- 8 sun-dried tomatoes, soaked in hot water, roughly chopped.
- 1 15 oz can have drained and rinsed kidney or other beans,
- 2-3 roughly chopped large leaves of Swiss chard.
- 1/3 cup of raw cashews; finely chopped.
- 1-2 cups of pasta sauce/tomato sauce

NUTRITIONAL INFORMATION:

Calories: 216 Kcal | Protein: 7.7 g | Carbohydrates: 34.9 g | Fat: 5.9 g | Fiber: 5.7 g

Prep. Time:	Total Time:	Servings:	Difficulty Level:
25 min.	55 min.	4	Medium

DIRECTIONS

Preheat the oven to 375 degrees Fahrenheit. For 5 minutes in boiling water, parboil the peppers.

In a big sauté pan with a small amount of water, sauté the onions. Add mushrooms and garlic and continue to simmer until nearly tender. Add and cook chard and beans until wilted. Add spaghetti sauce, sun-dried tomatoes, and 1 1/2 cups of rice. To mix, stir everything together.

Fill the pepper "cups" to the brim and garnish with chopped cashews. Cook for 20-25 minutes, covered until heated through. Remove the foil and cook the cashews for another 5-10 minutes.

STIR-FRIED ASPARAGUS WITH BELL PEPPERS AND CASHEW NUTS

INGREDIENTS

• 2 tablespoons of rice wine vinegar
• 3 tablespoons of vegetable broth; low sodium
• 2 tablespoons of hoisin sauce; gluten-free
• 3 tablespoons of balsamic vinegar
• 1 tablespoon of gluten-free, low, sodium tamari/soy sauce
• 1 teaspoon of toasted sesame oil
• 1 teaspoon of cornstarch
• 2 teaspoons of chili garlic sauce
• 1 cup of lightly chopped cashew nuts,
• 2 teaspoons of sugar
• 1 tablespoon of high oleic sunflower oil /other neutral vegetable oil
• 2 cups of chopped fresh asparagus: 1-inch pieces.
• 3 minced cloves garlic,
• 2 bell peppers; stems removed deseeded and chopped; 1-inch pieces.

NUTRITIONAL INFORMATION:

Calories: 302 kcal | Protein: 9 g | Carbohydrates: 25 g | Fat: 20 g | Fiber: 4 g

Prep. Time:	Total Time:	Servings:	Difficulty Level:
10 min.	20 min.	4	Easy

DIRECTIONS

To make the sauce, follow these steps: In a medium mixing bowl, combine the vinegar, sugar, broth, tamari, chili garlic sauce, hoisin sauce, and cornstarch. Stir everything together with a fork or a whisk until everything is thoroughly blended. Set it aside until you're ready to prepare the veggies. Bell peppers and asparagus should be prepared ahead of time. Set aside after chopping into 1-inch pieces. Garlic should be minced and put aside.

Cashew nuts should be chopped. On medium heat, warm a wok or a big cast iron pan. Add cashew nuts and cook for 2 to 3 minutes, stirring, until gently browned in a wok/skillet over medium heat. Remove the wok/skillet from the heat and place it in a bowl until ready. Add asparagus, sunflower/vegetable oil, and chopped garlic in a heated pan. Cook, stirring continuously, for 3 minutes over medium heat. Simmer for another 2 minutes after adding bell peppers, pour sauce over vegetables, and cook for another 2 to 3 minutes, or until sauce thickens. Add cashew nuts and sesame oil and divide into four servings. Enjoy while it's still warm.

VEGAN TACOS

INGREDIENTS

- 2 tablespoons of tamari/soy sauce; reduced sodium.
- 1 (16 ounces) package of drained, crumbled extra-firm tofu; patted dry
- ½ teaspoon of garlic powder
- 1 teaspoon of chili powder
- Pinch of salt
- ½ teaspoon of onion powder
- ½ cup of fresh salsa
- 1 tablespoon of olive oil; extra-virgin
- 2 cups of iceberg lettuce, shredded.
- 1 ripe avocado
- 8 corn /flour tortillas; warmed.
- 1 tablespoon of vegan mayonnaise
- Pickled radishes; for garnish
- 1 teaspoon of lime juice

NUTRITIONAL INFORMATION:

Calories: 360 Kcal | Protein: 16.6 g |
Carbohydrates: 32.6 g | Fat: 20.9 g | Fiber: 7.9 g

Prep. Time:	Total Time:	Servings:	Difficulty Level:
20 min.	20 min.	4	Medium

DIRECTIONS

In a medium mixing bowl, combine garlic powder, tamari/soy sauce, tofu, chili powder, and onion powder. In a large nonstick pan, heat the oil over medium-high heat. Cook, stirring periodically until the tofu mixture is well browned; it will take about 8 to 10 minutes.

In a small bowl, mash the avocado with lime juice, mayonnaise, and salt until smooth. In tortillas, serve the taco "meat" with salsa, avocado crema, and lettuce. If preferred, serve with pickled radishes on top.

Chapter 7:
Desserts

PUMPKIN BALLS

INGREDIENTS

- 1 oz chia seeds
- 4 oz crushed pumpkin seeds,
- 1 teaspoon of honey
- 5 chopped dates,

NUTRITIONAL INFORMATION:

Calories: 222 Kcal | Protein: 8.4 g | Carbohydrates: 17.3 g | Fat: 15.2 g | Fiber: 4.4 g

Prep. Time:	Total Time:	Servings:	Difficulty Level:
10 min.	10 min.	4	Easy

DIRECTIONS

In a mixing bowl, combine all ingredients and stir until smooth. Make balls out of the mixture and keep them refrigerated for up to 4 days.

MANGO PUDDING

INGREDIENTS

- 1 cup of plain Greek yogurt/ unsweetened
- 1 peeled mango; blended.
- 1 teaspoon of fresh mint
- 3 oz chia seeds

NUTRITIONAL INFORMATION:

Calories: 395 kcal | Protein: 15.4 g | Carbohydrates: 51.8 g | Fat: 15.2 g | Fiber: 17.4 g

Prep. Time:	Total Time:	Servings:	Difficulty Level:
10 min.	10 min.	2	Easy

DIRECTIONS

Combine the plain yogurt and chia seeds in the serving glasses. The yogurt is topped with pureed mango and fresh mint.

APPLE CHIPS

INGREDIENTS

- 1/2 tsp. of cinnamon
- 2 apples; thinly sliced
- 2 tsp. of honey

NUTRITIONAL INFORMATION:

Calories: 113 Kcal | Protein: 1 g | Carbohydrates: 30 g | Fat: 0 g | Fiber: 5 g

Prep. Time:	Total Time:	Servings:	Difficulty Level:
10 min.	3 hrs.	2	Easy

DIRECTIONS

Toss apples with honey and cinnamon in a large mixing bowl. Arrange apples in a single layer in an air fryer basket in batches (some overlap is okay). Cook at 350°F for 12 minutes, turning after every 4 minutes.

STRAWBERRY SHORTBREADS

INGREDIENTS

- ½ teaspoon of vanilla essence
- 400g strawberries
- 1 ½ tablespoons of icing sugar
- 100g coconut oil
- 200g thick coconut yogurt
- 80g banana
- 225g flour; gluten-free
- 50g sugar

NUTRITIONAL INFORMATION:

Calories: 120 Kcal | Protein: 3 g | Carbohydrates: 32 g | Fat: 11 g | Fiber: 3 g

Prep. Time:	Total Time:	Servings:	Difficulty Level:
20 min.	30 min.	4	Easy

DIRECTIONS

Preheat the oven to 180 degrees Celsius/160 degrees Celsius fan. Place half of the strawberries in a bowl and sprinkle with a teaspoon of icing sugar. While you're making the shortbread, put it in the fridge. Combine the sugar, coconut oil, and banana. Mix in the flour and make the dough. On a floured board, roll out the dough and cut out 16 circles using a pastry cutter. Cook for 12 minutes or until golden brown. Allow time for cooling. Combine the remaining icing sugar, the coconut yogurt, and the vanilla extract. Just before serving, put everything together. Place one shortbread circle on a plate, spread a couple of heaped teaspoons of coconut yogurt mixture over it, top with strawberries, and top with another shortbread circle. Using icing sugar, dust the cake. Repeat with the remaining shortbread, then top with the remaining strawberries.

FRESH FIG & BANANA SMOOTHIE

INGREDIENTS

- 1 1/2 cups of unsweetened almond milk
- 1 frozen banana
- 3-4 fresh figs; washed & stems removed and halved
- 1 teaspoon of vanilla extract
- Handful of ice
- 1 tablespoon of ground flaxseeds; optional

NUTRITIONAL INFORMATION:

Calories: 365 kcal | Protein: 9 g | Carbohydrates: 74 g | Fat: 7 g | Fiber: 9 g

Prep. Time:	Total Time:	Servings:	Difficulty Level:
5 min.	5 min.	2	Easy

DIRECTIONS

In a blender, combine all ingredients and mix until creamy and smooth. Serve right away! This dish also works nicely with frozen fresh figs.

GINGERBREAD DESSERT HUMMUS

INGREDIENTS

- 1/4 cup of Almond Butter; all natural
- 1 13.5 ounces rinsed and drained Can of Chickpeas
- 2 tablespoons of Blackstrap Molasses
- 3 tablespoons of Maple Syrup
- 2 teaspoons of Cinnamon Powder
- 1 teaspoon of Vanilla Extract
- 3/4 teaspoon of Ginger Powder
- 1 pinch of Salt
- 1/4 teaspoon of Ground Cloves

Prep. Time:	Total Time:	Servings:	Difficulty Level:
5 min.	10 min.	6	Easy

DIRECTIONS

In a food processor, combine all of the ingredients. Pulse until the chickpeas are integrated and the hummus has a smooth texture. Fill a dish with the dessert hummus and serve with gingerbread cookies, apples, or anything else you want. Serve.

NUTRITIONAL INFORMATION:

Calories: 236 kcal | Protein: 5 g | Carbohydrates: 40 g | Fat: 7 g | Fiber: 5 g

WATERMELON PIZZA

INGREDIENTS

- 2 large round slices of watermelon about 1 inch thick
- 3/4 cup of Low fat or fat-free plain Greek yogurt
- 1 teaspoon honey
- 1 tsp vanilla extract
- 1 cup fresh strawberries, sliced
- 1 cup fresh blackberries, sliced in half (You may use fresh blueberries if blackberries are unavailable. You can also use bananas or raspberries with, or instead, of strawberries)
- A handful of fresh mint leaves, rough chopped, optional

Prep. Time:	Total Time:	Servings:	Difficulty Level:
10 min.	10 min.	4	Easy

DIRECTIONS

Mix well with yogurt, honey, and vanilla in a bowl. Divide yogurt in half, and spread equal amounts on each watermelon round. Decorate each watermelon round with berries and sprinkle with mint leaves if using. Cut each watermelon round into 8 slices and serve.

NUTRITIONAL INFORMATION:

Calories: 150 Kcal | Protein: 10 g | Carbohydrates: 21 g | Fat: 4 g | Fiber: 2 g

CHOCOLATE AVOCADO PUDDING

INGREDIENTS

- 1/3 cup of raw cacao powder
- 2 large avocados; chilled
- 2 tsp of vanilla extract
- 1/2 cup of full-fat coconut milk
- 1/3 cup of maple syrup

Optional Toppings
- sea salt
- Hazelnuts; chopped

NUTRITIONAL INFORMATION:

Calories: 324 kcal | Protein: 6 g | Carbohydrates: 34 g | Fat: 23 g | Fiber: 13 g

Prep. Time:	Total Time:	Servings:	Difficulty Level:
5 min.	5 min.	4	Easy

DIRECTIONS

Remove the pit from the avocados and cut them in half. Fill a food processor halfway with flesh. Add remaining ingredients and stir well. Scrape down sides as required until the mixture is smooth and creamy. Check to see if you need to add any more sweetness. In four serving dishes, divide the chocolate avocado pudding. Serve with your preferred garnishes, such as hazelnuts & sea salt.

PINEAPPLE SORBE

INGREDIENTS

- 2 cups of chopped pineapple,
- 1 teaspoon of fresh mint
- 2 tablespoons of liquid honey

NUTRITIONAL INFORMATION:

Calories: 73 Kcal | Protein: 0.5 g | Carbohydrates: 19.5 g | Fat: 0.1 g | Fiber: 1.2 g

Prep. Time:	Total Time:	Servings:	Difficulty Level:
50 min.	55 min.	4	Medium

DIRECTIONS

Blend the pineapple until it is completely smooth. Mix in the liquid honey and the mint. The mixture should be stirred. Fill the silicone molds halfway with the mixture and freeze for 40 minutes. Then take the mixture from the molds into the processor and blend until smooth. Fill the serving dishes with dessert.

KIWI SORBET

INGREDIENTS

- 1 lime juiced
- 3 kiwis

NUTRITIONAL INFORMATION:

Calories: 93 kcal | Protein: 1 g | Carbohydrates: 23 g | Fat: 1 g | Fiber: 5 g

Prep. Time:	Total Time:	Servings:	Difficulty Level:
15 min.	15 min.	2	Easy

DIRECTIONS

Peel and slice the kiwis into rounds. Place the slices on a parchment-lined baking sheet and freeze until firm, for about 2-3 hours.

Add the fresh lime juice to the frozen kiwi slices in a food processor or high-powered blender. Pulse fruit until it achieves a sorbet-like consistency. You'll have to wipe the sides down a few times to attain uniformity.

Serve right now or freeze for later. If you freeze it, it will take 15 to 20 minutes to defrost enough to consume.

EASY ROASTED FRUIT

INGREDIENTS

- 1 1/2 cups of fresh blueberries
- 2 peaches, peeled & sliced
- 2 tablespoons of honey
- 1/8 teaspoon of ground cinnamon

NUTRITIONAL INFORMATION:

Calories: 199 kcal | Protein: 2.8 g | Carbohydrates: 39.7 g | Fat: 5.9 g | Fiber: 4.5 g

Prep. Time:	Total Time:	Servings:	Difficulty Level:
5 min.	30 min.	4	Medium

DIRECTIONS

Preheat the oven to 350 degrees Fahrenheit. In a baking dish, layer sliced peaches and blueberries. Cinnamon & brown sugar are sprinkled on top.

Bake for approximately 20 minutes at 350 degrees F, then reduce to a low broil setting and broil for about 5 mins or until bubbling. Allow to cool before serving, then cover and refrigerate.

ALMOND BUTTER AVOCADO FUDGSICLES

INGREDIENTS

Almond Butter Avocado Fudgsicles
- 2/3 cup of Cacao Powder
- 2 large Avocados, ripe
- 1 cup of full-fat Coconut Milk from a can
- 2 teaspoons of Liquid Stevia /2-3 tablespoons of maple syrup/honey; to taste
- Crushed almonds & flaky sea salt; for topping
- 1 teaspoon of Vanilla Extract
- Chocolate shell; for dipping
- 1/3 cup of Almond Butter

Chocolate Shell
- 1 teaspoon of Liquid Stevia /1 tablespoon of maple syrup/honey; to taste
- 1/2 cup of Coconut Oil; melted
- 1/4 cup of Cacao Powder

NUTRITIONAL INFORMATION:

Calories: 218 kcal | Protein: 4 g | Carbohydrates: 12 g | Fat: 20 g | Fiber: 8 g

Prep. Time:	Total Time:	Servings:	Difficulty Level:
30 min.	4 hrs. 30 min.	8	Medium

DIRECTIONS

Almond Butter Avocado Fudgsicles
Combine the cacao powder, avocados, vanilla extract, coconut milk, and liquid stevia (maple syrup/honey) in a food processor or high-powered blender. Blend until the mixture is smooth and creamy. Adjust the sweetness to your liking if necessary. In the chocolate fudge mixture, stir in the almond butter. Do not overmix the ingredients.

Fill popsicle molds halfway with almond butter fudge mixture. Make sure the fudge mixture goes to the bottom of the molds by tapping them on the counter a few times. Put a popsicle stick in the center of each slot and cover the popsicles with the lid (if you have one).

Place them in the freezer for at least 4 hours, preferably overnight. After the molds have been frozen, run them under cold Water for a few minutes to help the popsicles come out more readily. Remove the popsicles from the mold, coat them with chocolate (if desired), then sprinkle with sea salt and crushed almonds (optional). Serve and have fun!

Chocolate Shell
Combine the cacao powder, melted coconut oil, and stevia (honey /maple syrup) in a large mixing bowl. Adjust the sweetness to your liking if necessary.

Place the popsicles on parchment paper to harden after dipping them in the melted chocolate mixture. Serve and have fun!

GUAVA SMOOTHIE

INGREDIENTS

- 1 cup of chopped guava, seeds removed.
- 1 cup of finely chopped baby spinach.
- 1 tsp of fresh ginger, grated.
- ½ medium-sized peeled and chopped mango.
- 1 banana, peeled and sliced.
- 2 cups of Water

NUTRITIONAL INFORMATION:

Calories: 166 kcal | Protein: 3.9 g | Carbohydrates: 3 g | Fat: 1.4 g | Fiber: 7.8 g

Prep. Time:	Total Time:	Servings:	Difficulty Level:
5 min.	5-7 min.	2	Easy

DIRECTIONS

Cut the guava in half after peeling it. Wash it after scooping out the seeds. Set aside after cutting into small pieces. Under cold running water, thoroughly rinse the baby spinach. Drain well and rip into tiny pieces. Put it aside. Peel and cut the banana into tiny pieces. Put it aside. Cut the mango into tiny pieces after peeling it and put it aside. Mix the guava, banana, ginger, baby spinach, and mango in a juicer and process until smooth. Gradually drizzle in the Water and mix until everything is smooth and creamy. Before serving, transfer to serving glasses and chill for 20 minutes. Enjoy!

ORANGE GINGER TURMERIC SMOOTHIE

INGREDIENTS

- 1 large, chopped carrot
- 2 navel oranges; quartered and peeled
- 1-inch ginger piece; peeled
- Pinch of black pepper
- 1-inch turmeric piece; peeled

NUTRITIONAL INFORMATION:

Calories: 79 kcal | Protein: 2 g | Carbohydrates: 19 g | Fat: 1 g | Fiber: 4 g

Prep. Time:	Total Time:	Servings:	Difficulty Level:
5 min.	0 min.	2	Easy

DIRECTIONS

In a high-powered blender, combine all the ingredients, including 1 cup of ice cubes. Blend on high speed until completely smooth. For a more juice-like smoothie, add up to a cup of Water.

TURMERIC APPLE CIDER GINGER GUMMIES

INGREDIENTS

- 3 tablespoons of honey (maple syrup)
- 1 tablespoon of freshly grated ginger
- 1 teaspoon of ground turmeric
- 3 ½ tablespoons of grass-fed unflavored gelatin powder
- 1 ½ cups of apple cider vinegar
- 1 ½ cups of water; divided

NUTRITIONAL INFORMATION:

Calories: 5 kcal | Protein: 0 g | Carbohydrates: 2 g | Fat: 0 g | Fiber: 0 g

Prep. Time:	Total Time:	Servings:	Difficulty Level:
15 min.	4 hrs. 15 min.	8	Medium

DIRECTIONS

In a skillet over medium heat, combine honey, grated ginger, ground turmeric, apple cider vinegar, and 1 cup water. Let the mixture simmer for a few minutes. After straining the grated ginger bits out, turn off the heat in the skillet.

Add the gelatin powder gradually while stirring the remaining 1/2 cup water in a small bowl. Whisk the gelatin mixture until it is completely dissolved before adding it to the apple cider vinegar liquid.

Fill a 10" x 7" glass baking pan with the mixture. Wrap in plastic wrap, then refrigerate until firm (for 4 hours / overnight). Once set, cut into 3-inch squares that are enough to serve or keep for a week in the refrigerator.

Chapter 8:
Between Meals
Snacks

GRAIN-FREE BANANA GINGER BARS

INGREDIENTS

- ⅓ cup of coconut oil,
- 1 cup of coconut flour
- ⅓ cup of raw honey/ real maple syrup
- 2 tsp. of cinnamon
- 2 large/3 small ripe bananas
- 1½ Tbsp. of grated fresh ginger
- 6 eggs
- 1 tsp. of ground cardamom
- 2 tsp. of apple cider vinegar
- 1 tsp. of baking soda

NUTRITIONAL INFORMATION:

Calories: 205 Kcal | Protein: 8 g | Carbohydrates: 6.4 g | Fat: 8 g | Fiber: 2 g

Prep. Time:	Total Time:	Servings:	Difficulty Level:
45 min.	50 min.	4	Medium

DIRECTIONS

Preheat the oven to 350 degrees Fahrenheit. Grease or line a glass baking dish of 9x9 with parchment paper. Blend everything in a food processor until smooth, except the vinegar and baking soda. Add vinegar and baking soda in a blender until smooth, then pour into a prepared dish. Bake for 30-40 minutes or until a toothpick inserted in the center comes clean.

GARLIC PLANTAIN CHIPS

INGREDIENTS

- 2 tsp of garlic powder
- 3 cups of plantain chips
- 1 tbsp of lemon juice
- 3 tbsp of avocado oil or coconut oil

NUTRITIONAL INFORMATION:

Calories: 136 Kcal | Protein: 1 g | Carbohydrates: 17 g | Fat: 7 g | Fiber: 1 g

Prep. Time:	Total Time:	Servings:	Difficulty Level:
17 min.	20 min.	2	Easy

DIRECTIONS

Preheat the oven to 250 degrees Fahrenheit. Using parchment paper or Silpat, line a baking pan. Combine the coconut oil, plantain chips, and garlic in a large mixing bowl. Toss the chips lightly with your hands so that they are equally covered. When the oven is heated, pour in the lemon juice, and mix it in.

On the prepared baking pan, spread out the seasoned plantain chips. Bake for 12 minutes or until just starting to brown, then drain on a paper towel for a minute or two to absorb any leftover oil before eating.

PUMPKIN PIE GRANOLA

INGREDIENTS

- ¼ teaspoon of nutmeg
- ⅓ cup of pumpkin seeds
- ¼ teaspoon of salt
- 1/2 teaspoon of pumpkin pie spice
- 1/4 cup of pumpkin puree
- 1/2 teaspoon of cinnamon
- 1/4 cup of agave
- 1 1/2 cups of oats
- Vegetable or Canola oil cooking spray
- 1/4 cup of canola or vegetable oil

NUTRITIONAL INFORMATION:

Calories: 164.2 Kcal | Protein: 3 g | Carbohydrates: 16.1 g | Fat: 10.8 g | Fiber: 3 g

Prep. Time:	Total Time:	Servings:	Difficulty Level:
30 min.	35 min.	5	Medium

DIRECTIONS

Preheat the oven to 325 degrees Fahrenheit. Mix the oats, salt, spices, and pumpkin seeds in a large bowl. Combine the oil, agave, and pumpkin puree in a separate dish.

Stir in the pumpkin mixture with oats and spices. The mixture must be wet and uniformly covered. Spray a baking sheet with nonstick cooking spray. Using a spatula, evenly distribute the oat mixture onto the baking sheet. Bake for about 10 minutes in the oven. Remove the pan from the oven and swirl it around. Bake for another 10 minutes or until the granola is golden and crispy.

MINTED BABA GHANOUSH

INGREDIENTS

- juice of 1 lime
- 3 medium eggplants
- 1 teaspoon of ground coriander
- 1/2 cup of tahini
- 1 teaspoon of salt
- 2 minced garlic cloves
- 1 tablespoon of olive oil
- 2 tablespoons of chopped mint leaves

NUTRITIONAL INFORMATION:

Calories: 85 Kcal | Protein: 2.9 g | Carbohydrates: 11.3 g | Fat: 4.3 g | Fiber: 5 g

Prep. Time:	Total Time:	Servings:	Difficulty Level:
10 min.	55 min.	4	Easy

DIRECTIONS

Preheat the oven to 375 degrees Fahrenheit. Poke the eggplants with a fork and roast for 45 minutes on foil on a baking sheet. Allow it to cool for 10 minutes before halving the eggplants vertically, scooping off the flesh, and straining it through a fine-mesh strainer.

Press out the fluid and drain it. Then, using a food processor or blender, puree the flesh. Remove the skin and throw it away. Add coriander, garlic, tahini, lime juice, and salt. Blend for approximately 2 minutes or until smooth. Garnish with olive oil and mint before serving.

BLACK BEAN BROWNIES

INGREDIENTS

- 1/2 cup of semisweet chocolate chips; divided.
- 1 can (15 ounces) of rinsed and drained black beans,
- 1/2 teaspoon of baking powder
- 2/3 cup of packed brown sugar
- 3 tablespoons of canola oil
- 1/2 cup of baking cocoa
- 3 large eggs; room temperature
- 1/8 teaspoon of sea salt
- 1 teaspoon of vanilla extract

NUTRITIONAL INFORMATION:

Calories: 167 Kcal | Protein: 4 g | Carbohydrates: 24 g | Fat: 7 g | Fiber: 2 g

Prep. Time:	Total Time:	Servings:	Difficulty Level:
25 min.	45 min.	6	Medium

DIRECTIONS

In a food processor, combine the 1/4 cup of chocolate chips, beans, and oil, cover, and process until smooth. Add brown sugar, eggs, cocoa, baking powder, vanilla, and salt and blend until smooth.

Transfer to an 8-inch square baking sheet lined with parchment paper. The leftover chocolate chips may be sprinkled on top. Bake for 20-25 minutes or until a tester inserted in the middle comes clean. Allow it to cool on a wire rack, and slice it into bars.

NUTS AND SEEDS TRAIL MIX

INGREDIENTS

- 1 cup of unblanched almonds
- 1 cup of salted pumpkin seeds/pepitas
- 1 cup of walnut halves
- 1 cup of unsalted sunflower kernels
- 1 cup of dark chocolate chips
- 1 cup of dried apricots

NUTRITIONAL INFORMATION:

Calories: 85 Kcal | Protein: 2.9 g | Carbohydrates: 11.3 g | Fat: 4.3 g | Fiber: 5 g

Prep. Time:	Total Time:	Servings:	Difficulty Level:
5 min.	5 min.	4 cups	Easy

DIRECTIONS

Toss all of the ingredients together in a large mixing bowl. Keep the container sealed.

SLOW COOKER APPLESAUCE

INGREDIENTS

- 1/2 cup of water
- 1/3 cup of brown sugar or organic cane sugar
- 10 Honeycrisp apples; 12 cups of sliced apples
- 1/3 teaspoon of cinnamon
- 1/2 Tablespoon of lemon juice

NUTRITIONAL INFORMATION:

Calories: 201 Kcal | Protein: 1 g | Carbohydrates: 53 g | Fat: 1 g | Fiber: 7 g

Prep. Time:	Total Time:	Servings:	Difficulty Level:
10 min.	5 hrs. 15 min.	6	Easy

DIRECTIONS

Place the apples in a slow cooker after peeling and thinly slicing them. Add sugar, lemon juice, water, and cinnamon. Cook for 5-6 hours on low or until apples is mushy and supple. You may mash the apples with a potato masher for the applesauce to be chunky. You may purée it with the immersion blender if you want it to be smooth.

GRILLED EGGPLANT PROVOLONE

INGREDIENTS

- ¼ teaspoon of dried oregano
- 3 tablespoons of olive oil
- ½ teaspoon of kosher salt
- Four small eggplants, half lengthwise
- 1½ tablespoons of balsamic vinegar
- Black pepper; freshly ground.
- Grilled Salsa
- ½ pound of mild provolone; thick-sliced.

NUTRITIONAL INFORMATION:

Calories: 196 Kcal | Protein: 9 g | Carbohydrates: 13 g | Fat: 13 g | Fiber: 7 g

Prep. Time:	Total Time:	Servings:	Difficulty Level:
30 min.	45 min.	8	Easy

DIRECTIONS

Brush the sliced sides of the eggplants with a mixture of oil, vinegar, and oregano. Season to taste with pepper and salt. Preheat the gas grill to high; after 15 minutes, reduce the heat to medium. (If using charcoal, cook until the coals are completely coated with grey ash.) Grill eggplants cut-side down for approximately 5 minutes or until browned. Top each half of the eggplant with a piece of provolone. For 3 minutes longer, grill them or until the cheese is bubbling. Serve with a side of Grilled Salsa.

Aperitifs

TANGERINE GINGER JUICE

INGREDIENTS

- 4 tangerines
- 1 cup of carrots
- 1/2 teaspoon of ginger

NUTRITIONAL INFORMATION:

Calories: 239 kcal | Protein: 4 g | Carbohydrates: 59 g | Fat: 1 g | Fiber: 9 g

Prep. Time:	Total Time:	Servings:	Difficulty Level:
20 min.	5 min.	4	Easy

DIRECTIONS

Remove the peels from the ginger and oranges. In a juicer, juice the tangerines and carrots. The ginger will probably juice nicely in a high-powered juicer. If this is not the case, go to the next step. Extract ginger juice and add it to the liquid using a garlic press.

CELERY JUICE

INGREDIENTS

- 1 cup of water
- 3 to 4 bunches of celery

NUTRITIONAL INFORMATION:

Calories: 33 kcal | Protein: 2 g | Carbohydrates: 7 g | Fat: 0.44 g | Fiber: 4 g

Prep. Time:	Total Time:	Servings:	Difficulty Level:
5 min.	15 min.	1	Easy

DIRECTIONS

Cut celery into more manageable bits. Blender with water and celery that has been chopped. When necessary, add extra water until creamy, and blend. Place a pitcher on top of a nut milk bag. Add celery juice that has been pureed to the nut milk bag. Squeeze the drink through the bag with your hands.

DILUTED APPLE CIDER VINEGAR

INGREDIENTS

- 2 tbsp apple cider vinegar
- 1 glass of water

NUTRITIONAL INFORMATION:

Calories: 0 kcal | Protein: 0 g | Carbohydrates: 0 g | Fat: 0 g | Fiber: 0 g

Prep. Time:	Total Time:	Servings:	Difficulty Level:
5 min.	5 min.	1	Easy

DIRECTIONS

In a glass full of water, add the apple cider vinegar. Mix well and consume it slowly. Drinking the whole glass at once can cause acidity.

CUCUMBER WATER

INGREDIENTS

- 1 cucumber sliced.
- 1 lemon slice.
- 2 cups water

NUTRITIONAL INFORMATION:

Calories: 3 kcal | Protein: 0.2 g | Carbohydrates: 0.5 g | Fat: 0 g | Fiber: 0.2 g

Prep. Time:	Total Time:	Servings:	Difficulty Level:
5 min.	5 min.	1	Easy

DIRECTIONS

In a wide-mouth bottle, add the cucumber and lemon slices. Slightly warm the water and pour it into the bottle with the slices. Refrigerate for 1 or 2 hours and consume throughout the day.

APPLE-CINNAMON FLAVORED WATER

INGREDIENTS

- 2 tsp of ground cinnamon
- 10 cups of water
- 2 cinnamon sticks
- 1 medium apple

NUTRITIONAL INFORMATION:

Calories: 16 kcal | Protein: 0 g | Carbohydrates: 4 g | Fat: 0 g | Fiber: 0 g

Prep. Time:	Total Time:	Servings:	Difficulty Level:
10 min.	10 min.	10	Easy

DIRECTIONS

Slice the apple into small pieces without peeling. Use a pitcher to add all the ingredients. Before serving, refrigerator overnight.

GREEN JUICE

INGREDIENTS

- 1 cucumber: medium
- 1/2 lemon
- 2 green apples: medium
- 1/2 cup of fresh pineapple

NUTRITIONAL INFORMATION:

Calories: 130 kcal | Protein: 1 g | Carbohydrates: 31 g | Fat: 1 g | Fiber: 0 g

Prep. Time:	Total Time:	Servings:	Difficulty Level:
5 min.	5 min.	2	Easy

DIRECTIONS

Clean all ingredients well and cut apple and cucumber into cubes. Extract juice using a juicer and drink fresh.

BEET AND APPLE JUICE BLEND

INGREDIENTS

- 1/4 cup of parsley
- 1 medium fresh carrot: medium
- 1/2 apple: medium
- 1 celery stalk
- 1/2 beet: medium

NUTRITIONAL INFORMATION:

Calories: 53 kcal | Protein: 1 g | Carbohydrates: 13 g | Fat: 0 g | Fiber: 0 g

Prep. Time:	Total Time:	Servings:	Difficulty Level:
5 min.	5 min.	2	Easy

DIRECTIONS

In a juicer, put the beet, apple, celery, parsley, and carrot; process them for juice extraction. Drink it fresh or put it to cool in the refrigerator.

STRAWBERRY SORBET

INGREDIENTS

- 1 tbsp of lemon juice
- 4 tbsp of honey
- 1 ¼ cups of crushed or cubed ice.
- ¼ cup of water
- 1 cup of frozen or fresh strawberries, cleaned

NUTRITIONAL INFORMATION:

Calories: 22 kcal | Protein: 0 g | Carbohydrates: 5 g | Fat: 0 g | Fiber: 1.5 g

Prep. Time:	Total Time:	Servings:	Difficulty Level:
5 min.	5 min.	4	Easy

DIRECTIONS

Blend all the ingredients for sorbet in a blender until it forms a smooth texture.

Herbal Teas

PEPPERMINT TEA

INGREDIENTS

- 1/2 cup dried Peppermint Leaf
- 4 cups of hot water

Prep. Time:	Total Time:	Servings:	Difficulty Level:
5 min.	15 min.	4	Easy

NUTRITIONAL INFORMATION:

Calories: 34.2 kcal | Protein: 0.1 g | Carbohydrates: 0 g | Fat: 0 g | Fiber: 0 g

DIRECTIONS

Set Water to boil. Once boiling, add peppermint leaves and remove them from the heat. Cover and let rest for at least 5 minutes. Strain, serve, and enjoy.

ALMOND TEA

INGREDIENTS

- 5 Tbsp. Almond powder
- 1 cup Water
- 1 tsp. Cinnamon

Prep. Time:	Total Time:	Servings:	Difficulty Level:
5 min.	5 min.	2-3	Easy

NUTRITIONAL INFORMATION:

Calories: 40 kcal | Protein: 1.5 g | Carbohydrates: 1.4 g | Fat: 3 g | Fiber: 2 g

DIRECTIONS

Boil water with all ingredients. Serve warmly.

CHAMOMILE TEA

INGREDIENTS

- 2 cups Water
- 3 teaspoons Dried Chamomile

Prep. Time:	Total Time:	Servings:	Difficulty Level:
5 min.	5 min.	2	Easy

NUTRITIONAL INFORMATION:

Calories: 1 kcal | Protein: 0 g | Carbohydrates: 0.4 g | Fat: 0 g | Fiber: 0.7 g

DIRECTIONS

Bring water to a boil in a pot over high heat. As soon as the water begins to boil, turn off the heat and add dried Chamomile. Keep the lid on for one minute. Pour the chamomile tea through a strainer into the teacups, stir it up, and serve.

TURMERIC TEA

INGREDIENTS

- 1 handful of cilantro; chopped
- 32 oz boiling water
- 1 Tbsp of olive oil
- ½ Tbsp of turmeric powder
- 1 garlic clove; peeled & crushed
- 2 lemons; juiced
- 1 Tbsp of fresh ginger; thinly sliced
- 1 orange; juiced (or 1½ tbsp of honey)
- 5 peppercorns; whole

NUTRITIONAL INFORMATION:

Calories: 26.8 kcal | Protein: 0.1 g | Carbohydrates: 6.8 g | Fat: 0 g | Fiber: 0 g

Prep. Time:	Total Time:	Servings:	Difficulty Level:
10 min.	20 min.	4	Easy

DIRECTIONS

Heat water in a saucepan and then stir in the remaining ingredients. Serve hot.

HERBAL TEA

INGREDIENTS

- 5 cup water
- ¼ tsp clove powder
- 1 tsp fennel seeds
- 5 green cardamoms
- 10 mint leaves
- ¼ tsp ginger powder

NUTRITIONAL INFORMATION:

Calories: 37 kcal | Protein: 0.4 g | Carbohydrates: 7 g | Fat: 0.7 g | Fiber: 0.3 g

Prep. Time:	Total Time:	Servings:	Difficulty Level:
2 min.	10 min.	2	Easy

DIRECTIONS

In a saucepan, bring water to a boil. Add all the herbs and boil for 2 minutes. Turn off the flame and cover the saucepan for 5 minutes so the herbs can infuse. Strain the tea in another saucepan and bring it to a boil. Serve hot.

LEMON GRASS TEA

INGREDIENTS

- 2 sticks of lemongrass
- 1 lemon
- 1 ½ cup water

Prep. Time:	Total Time:	Servings:	Difficulty Level:
2 min.	10 min.	2	Easy

NUTRITIONAL INFORMATION:

Calories: 1.8 kcal | Protein: 0 g | Carbohydrates: 0.5 g | Fat: 0 g | Fiber: 0 g

DIRECTIONS

In a small saucepan, add water and add lemongrass. Bring the water to a boil and lower the flame. Let it simmer for 5 to 6 mins. Turn off the flame and strain the tea into your cup. Squeeze a lemon in the tea to enhance flavor. Enjoy your tea.

PEACH TEA

INGREDIENTS

- 2 tsp dried peach bits
- 1 lemon
- 1 ½ cup water

Prep. Time:	Total Time:	Servings:	Difficulty Level:
2 min.	10 min.	2	Easy

NUTRITIONAL INFORMATION:

Calories: 0 kcal | Protein: 0 g | Carbohydrates: 1 g | Fat: 0 g | Fiber: 0 g

DIRECTIONS

In a small saucepan, add water and dried peach bits. Bring the water to a boil and lower the flame. Let it simmer for 5 to 6 mins. Turn off the flame and strain the tea into your cup. Squeeze a lemon in the tea to enhance flavor. Enjoy your tea.

JASMINE TEA

INGREDIENTS

- 1 tsp dried jasmine flowers
- 1 ½ cup water
- Few mints leaves

Prep. Time:	Total Time:	Servings:	Difficulty Level:
2 min.	15 min.	2	Easy

NUTRITIONAL INFORMATION:

Calories: 56.2 kcal | Protein: 0 g | Carbohydrates: 17 g | Fat: 0 g | Fiber: 0 g

DIRECTIONS

In a saucepan, put water, jasmine tea, and mint leaves. Bring the water to a boil. Boil for 2 minutes and turn off the stove. Cover the saucepan and let the tea infuse. After 10 minutes, turn on the flame and boil it. As soon as the tea boils, strain it into your cup and enjoy it.

Herbs

ITALIAN SEASONING

INGREDIENTS

- 1 tbsp of Dried Thyme
- 2 tbsp of Dried Oregano
- 1 tbsp of Dried Rosemary
- 1 tbsp of Dried Marjoram
- 2 tbsp of Dried Basil

NUTRITIONAL INFORMATION:

Calories: 17.5 kcal | Protein: 0.8 g | Carbohydrates: 3.9 g | Fat: 0.3 g | Fiber: 1.7 g

Prep. Time:	Total Time:	Servings:	Difficulty Level:
5 min.	5 min.	6	Easy

DIRECTIONS

Combine oregano, Basil, garlic powder, onion powder, parsley, and black Pepper. Store it in an airtight jar.

ALL-PURPOSE NO-SALT SEASONING MIX

INGREDIENTS

- 1¼ teaspoon ground thyme
- 1 teaspoon ground mace
- 1 tablespoon garlic powder
- 1½ teaspoons dried parsley
- 1½ teaspoons dried Basil
- 1 teaspoon ground black pepper
- 1 teaspoon onion powder
- 1¼ teaspoon dried savory
- ¼ teaspoon cayenne pepper
- 1 teaspoon dried sage

NUTRITIONAL INFORMATION:

Calories: 20.7 kcal | Protein:1 g | Carbohydrates: 3.7 g | Fat: 1 g | Fiber: 1.5 g

Prep. Time:	Total Time:	Servings:	Difficulty Level:
5 min.	5 min.	10	Easy

DIRECTIONS

Mix Basil, garlic powder, parsley, thyme, savory, onion powder, mace, sage, cayenne Pepper, and Black Pepper, and reserve it in a covered jar.

GARLIC-HERB SEASONING

INGREDIENTS

- 1 tsp Powdered lemon rind
- 2 tsp Garlic powder
- 1 tsp Oregano
- 1 tsp Basil

NUTRITIONAL INFORMATION:

Calories: 5.2 kcal | Protein: 0.2 g | Carbohydrates: 1 g | Fat: 0.2 g | Fiber: 0.4 g

Prep. Time:	Total Time:	Servings:	Difficulty Level:
5 min.	5 min.	6	Easy

DIRECTIONS

In a processor, combine ingredients. Store rice grains to avoid clumping in a sealed jar.

POULTRY SEASONING

INGREDIENTS

- 1 tsp black pepper: ground
- 2 tbsp ground sage: dried
- 2 tsp dried marjoram
- 2 tsp dried thyme

NUTRITIONAL INFORMATION:

Calories: 13.5 kcal | Protein: 0.4 g | Carbohydrates: 2.9 g | Fat: 0.3 g | Fiber: 0.5 g

Prep. Time:	Total Time:	Servings:	Difficulty Level:
3 min.	3 min.	5	Easy

DIRECTIONS

In a small bowl, combine all ingredients. Add this blend to an airtight jar. Good to use for one year.

ANTI-INFLAMMATORY OIL

INGREDIENTS

- 1 tablespoon of dried thyme
- ¼ cup of olive oil
- 1 peeled garlic clove,
- 2 tablespoons of dried rosemary

NUTRITIONAL INFORMATION:

Calories: 116 kcal | Protein: 0.2 g | Carbohydrates: 1.7 g | Fat: 12.9 g | Fiber: 1 g

Prep. Time:	Total Time:	Servings:	Difficulty Level:
10 min.	10 min.	4	Easy

DIRECTIONS

Close the lid on the can after adding all of the ingredients. Refrigerate oil for 1-2 days.

SAMBAL OELEK

INGREDIENTS

- 1 tablespoon of salt
- 2 tablespoons of rice vinegar
- 1 pound of red chili peppers; stems removed.

NUTRITIONAL INFORMATION:

Calories: 9 kcal | Protein: 0.1 g | Carbohydrates: 2 g | Fat: 0 g | Fiber: 0.1 g

Prep. Time:	Total Time:	Servings:	Difficulty Level:
5 min.	10 min.	6	Easy

DIRECTIONS

In a food processor or equivalent grinder, combine all of the ingredients. A Molcajete is an excellent choice for this. Grind until you get a coarse paste. If you want to, strain off some of the extra liquid. Cover and place in a jar. Keep it refrigerated until you're ready to use it.

HOT KETCHUP

INGREDIENTS

- 1 minced jalapeno pepper,
- 1 teaspoon of dried Basil
- 2 cups of chopped tomatoes,
- 1 minced chili pepper,
- 1 teaspoon of minced garlic

NUTRITIONAL INFORMATION:

Calories: 19 kcal | Protein: 0.9 g | Carbohydrates: 4 g | Fat: 0.2 g | Fiber: 1.2 g

Prep. Time:	Total Time:	Servings:	Difficulty Level:
10 min.	15 min.	4	Easy

DIRECTIONS

Pour the tomatoes into the pot after blending them into a smooth paste. Add garlic, dried Basil, jalapeño pepper, and chili pepper. Bring the ketchup to a boil in a saucepan.

MUSTARD DRESSING

INGREDIENTS

- 3 tablespoons of lemon juice
- 3 tablespoons of mustard
- 1 egg, beaten.

NUTRITIONAL INFORMATION:

Calories: 58 kcal | Protein: 3.6 g | Carbohydrates: 3.3 g | Fat: 3.6 g | Fiber: 1.3 g

Prep. Time:	Total Time:	Servings:	Difficulty Level:
10 min.	10 min.	4	Easy

DIRECTIONS

The egg should be whisked. Add lemon juice and mustard. Combine the dressing ingredients well.

CONCLUSION

Our potential and lifespan are affected by our diet. Many workers get home after work hours, exhausted and with few eating alternatives because of the busy nature of the job. Many of us suffer from allergies made worse by weather or surroundings changes. Inflammation levels, for instance, are especially high in the winter, which, if left untreated, may throw the body out of balance and increase the risk of diseases, including diabetes, cancer, heart disease, arthritis, and joint pain, as well as chronic inflammation. Primarily, you may reduce inflammation by consuming less processed foods, red meats, and alcoholic beverages.

Fruits and vegetables may be substituted. After making dietary adjustments, you'll need to learn how to prepare and consume wholesome anti-inflammatory foods. Foods that will improve your immune system should be consumed since it is crucial. For your friends, family, and other loved ones, this would motivate you to prepare wholesome meals. After consuming anti-inflammatory meals, you'll feel more energetic and far less worn out.

Making a sudden transformation after becoming used to an unhealthy eating habit may be challenging but worthwhile. Wellness-promoting meals (described in this book) might improve your thinking and memory. All that is required is a determined mindset. You may wish to help your family members get the benefits of whole foods and teach them to always eat a balanced diet. Like poor food, meals that fight inflammation and chronic illness don't need to be hurried. As previously said, a sudden change could be difficult, but if you concentrate on the advantages as others did, you'll see that it's worthwhile.

Meal preparation takes place on the weekends when you have a hectic workweek. Prepare food for the week by making a grocery list before going to the store, shopping on Saturdays, and cooking on Sundays. There are wholesome, batch-friendly recipes in this book. The recipes are designed to make consuming anti-inflammatory foods simple. To store in the fridge and reheat over the week, you may double or quadruple the component amounts. You can prepare meals, consume them, and feel as healthy as you did a few years ago with the help of this book.

4 WEEKS MEAL PLAN

The meal plan for reducing inflammation comprised 3 meals & three snacks with a healthy ratio of carbohydrates, protein, and fat. Each meal has between 400 and 500 calories, while each snack has 150 and 300 calories.

It's OK to substitute food since this meal plan is just designed to be a suggestion. To avoid significant changes to the nutritional profile of meals or snacks, strive to keep the replacement food items equal.

For instance, swapping grilled salmon for roasted chicken won't significantly change the nutritional profile. However, substituting fried fish for grilled salmon increases the number of calories, carbohydrates, and fat. Here is an example of 5 meals with calorie proportion.

Breakfast (330 calories)
Baby Kale Breakfast Salad with Quinoa & Strawberries

A.M. Snack (131 calories)
1 large pear

Lunch (416 calories)
Curried Chickpea Lettuce Wraps

P.M. Snack (105 calories)
8 walnut halves

Dinner (356 calories)
Zoodles & Grilled Shrimp with the Lemon Basil Dressing

To make 1,200 calories: Change A.M. snack to 1/2 cup sliced cucumbers, substitute Green Salads at lunch, and change P.M. snack to 1 clementine.

To make 2,000 calories: Breakfast must have 1 medium orange. The morning snack should include 1/3 cup of unsalted dry-roasted almonds, & afternoon snack should include 1/4 cup of walnuts & 1 medium apple.

While you make dietary changes, a meal plan provides support. The recipes are part of the meal plan, so you can keep eating healthy daily. You can remain on schedule, save money, prepare quickly, save time, and reduce waste with the help of these meal plans. This 28-day meal plan aims to ease some unpredictability associated with preparing meals and grocery shopping.

Week 1

Days	Mon	Tue	Wed	Thu	Fri	Sat	Sun
Breakfast	Chia Pudding	Zucchini Oatmeal	Mexican Breakfast Hash	Homemade Muesli	Spanish omelet	Southwest Tofu Scramble	Chamomile and Maple Porridge
Lunch	Broccoli Soup	Vegan Roasted Pumpkin Curry	Superfood Baked Salmon	Chicken, Avocado & Quinoa Bowls with Herb Dressing	Mediterranean Grilled Eggplant Salad	Celery Root Salad	Sweet & Sour Chicken
Dinner	Garlic Salmon	Turmeric Lime Chicken	Carrot Ginger Soup	Curried Chickpea Lettuce Wraps	Creamy Leek & Salmon Soup	Chicken Teriyaki Rice	Vegan Tacos

Week 2

Days	Mon	Tue	Wed	Thu	Fri	Sat	Sun
Breakfast	Spanish omelet	Anti-inflammatory Smoothie	Fresh Turmeric Smoothie Bowl	Fertility-Boosting Pudding Parfait	Apple-Cinnamon Overnight Oats	Fresh Turmeric Smoothie Bowl	Zucchini Oatmeal
Lunch	Curry Tofu	Instant Pot Potato Leek Soup	Superfood Baked Salmon	White Bean and Chicken Chili Blanca	Vegan Tacos	Superfood Baked Salmon	Thai Green Curry with Shrimp and Kale
Dinner	Mango Shrimp Kebabs	Fish Ceviche	Curried Chickpea Lettuce Wraps	Blackened Salmon	Roasted Salmon with Smoky Chickpeas & Greens	Curried Chickpea Lettuce Wraps	Kung Pao Chicken

Week 3

Days	Mon	Tue	Wed	Thu	Fri	Sat	Sun
Breakfast	Anti-inflammatory Smoothie	Sweet Potato Toast	Fertility-Boosting Pudding Parfait	Fresh Turmeric Smoothie Bowl	Anti-inflammatory Smoothie	Homemade Muesli	Mexican Breakfast Hash
Lunch	Instant Pot Potato Leek Soup	Curry Tofu	White Bean and Chicken Chili Blanca	Superfood Baked Salmon	Instant Pot Potato Leek Soup	Chicken, Avocado & Quinoa Bowls with Herb Dressing	Superfood Baked Salmon
Dinner	Fish Ceviche	Fish Ceviche	Blackened Salmon	Curried Chickpea Lettuce Wraps	Fish Ceviche	Curried Chickpea Lettuce Wraps	Carrot Ginger Soup

Week 4

Days	Mon	Tue	Wed	Thu	Fri	Sat	Sun
Breakfast	Chia Pudding	Sweet Potato Toast	Mexican Breakfast Hash	Zucchini Oatmeal	Anti-inflammatory Smoothie	Spanish omelet	Mexican Breakfast Hash
Lunch	Broccoli Soup	Curry Tofu	Superfood Baked Salmon	Vegan Roasted Pumpkin Curry	Instant Pot Potato Leek Soup	Mediterranean Grilled Eggplant Salad	Superfood Baked Salmon
Dinner	Garlic Salmon	Fish Ceviche	Carrot Ginger Soup	Boiled Chicken	Fish Ceviche	Creamy Leek & Salmon Soup	Carrot Ginger Soup

Measuring Conversions

There are two widely employed measuring schemes in nutrition: Metric and US Customary.

Dry Measure Equivalent

3 teaspoons	1/2 ounce	1 tablespoon	14.3 grams
2 tablespoons	1 ounce	1/8 cup	28.3 grams
4 tablespoons	2 ounces	1/4 cup	56.7 grams
5 1/3 tablespoons	2.6 ounces	1/3 cup	75.6 grams
8 tablespoons	4 ounces	1/2 cup	113.4 grams
12 tablespoons	6 ounces	3/4 cup	.375 pound
32 tablespoons	16 ounces	2 cups	1 pound

Weight (mass)	
Metric (grams)	**US contemporary (ounces)**
14 grams	1/2 ounce
28 grams	1 ounce
85 grams	3 ounces
100 grams	3.53 ounces
113 grams	4 ounces
227 grams	8 ounces
340 grams	12 ounces
454 grams	16 ounces or 1 pound

Volume (liquid)

Metric	US Customary
.6 ml	1/8 tsp
1.2 ml	1/4 tsp
2.5 ml	1/2 tsp
3.7 ml	3/4 tsp
5 ml	1 tsp
15 ml	1 tbsp
30 ml	2 tbsp
59 ml	2 fluid ounces or1/4 cup
118 ml	1/2 cup
177 ml	3/4 cup
237 ml	1 cup or 8 fluid ounces
1.9 liters	8 cups or 1/2 gallon

Oven Temperatures	
Metric	**US contemporary**
121° C	250° F
149° C	300° F
177° C	350° F
204° C	400° F
232° C	450° F

BONUS

The advice contained in this book is the result, above all, of my university and professional studies and the knowledge gained during over 40 years of sports school teaching, as well as of my mother and grandmother always looking for healthy and tasty ways and recipes, carefully selected for providing the best supply of nutrients to my children, first, and to my grandchildren, then, whose growth and development I have daily monitored, both physical and mental, to help them to be people who are always healthy and with a correct and functional diet.

It is not possible, with a single book, to contain all the human knowledge related to the science of nutrition, but I am sure that starting to follow simple food rules and a healthy lifestyle can start with small steps taken in the right direction.

You will discover, following the advice contained in the book with confidence, that maintaining a correct diet is very easy and fun, as well as stimulating because you will find yourself having a feeling of well-being and energy in your body that you had lost for some time or that you did not think was possible.

To help you along this path, I thought it would be very useful and pleasant to have the help and stimulus of other people who, like you, have decided to think about their bodies, their health, and that of the loved ones around you.

I have therefore added these 4 BONUSES to my book so that you will have:

1) A Facebook group where you can come into direct contact with me and with other people who, like you, are following a correct and healthy diet, asking for advice and exchanging ideas and recipes, receiving support for every need, or even, quite simply, support and encouragement to move forward most correctly.
2) An exercise plan is simple and easy to do, even at home or near your home, which will help you amplify the effects of your correct diet excitingly.
3) A nice planner to plan your weekly food plan, including always new and tasty recipes every day, complete with a space for the shopping list that will help you buy only what you need while saving money and staying within your budget
4) Finally, I have included a nice challenge in 30 days, in which you will start measuring your results and touch the extraordinary effects of a healthy diet, which will provide your body with an enormous amount of energy

I'll wait for you in the Facebook group to get to know us and make the most of the benefits of a healthy diet and a positive and motivating community.

Click NOW on the group link that you find written here:

https://www.facebook.com/groups/691373446108954/

Private FB group with tips, new recipes, challenge participants, exercises

Join the private group on Facebook to receive suggestions, and new recipes, challenge the participants, exercises

https://www.facebook.com/groups/691373446108954/

Weekly planner and shopping list – save budget

you can download it from the resources of the Facebook group

E-book challenge 30 days to get back in shape

you can download it from the resources of the Facebook group

Light exercise plan eBook

you can download it from the resources of the Facebook group

34532572R00063